"This is an incredible story!"

Steve Harvey, media mogul, Emmy Award–winning
comedian, and *New York Times* bestselling author

"Sam is no stranger to our stages. We've been inspired by his
story. I'm honored Sam calls North Point home."

Andy Stanley, founder of North Point Ministries

"The minute I met Sam, I called everyone I knew and said,
'You've got to have this guy speak at your event.' Eight years
later, I'm still telling people to check out Sam."

Jon Acuff, *New York Times* bestselling author

"Sam has helped us tremendously at Reach Records. I'm sure
anything he writes is a must-read."

Lecrae, Grammy Award–winning recording artist

"Sam has an opportunity to bridge a racial divide in the church.
Maybe that's a part of the greater story here as well. His story
is incredible."

Jeff Henderson, founder of Preaching Rocket
and lead pastor at Gwinnett Church

"Sam's story is one of adversity and triumph, humility and
learning, brokenness and building. I'm grateful that he is
willing to give so many of us a window into the pivotal moments that have shaped him. Those of us who know Sam are
inspired by his resilience, his passion to be a winner, and his
drive to show others that they have a greater story to tell too."

Reggie Joiner, founder and CEO of Orange

"I want to read anything Sam Collier writes because he is an
empowering leader who offers fresh insight and prophetic
instruction for living our best lives!!"

Danielle Strickland, international speaker, author,
and global social justice advocate

A
GREATER
STORY

. . .

MY RESCUE, YOUR PURPOSE,
AND OUR PLACE IN GOD'S PLAN

SAM COLLIER

BakerBooks

a division of Baker Publishing Group
Grand Rapids, Michigan

Published by Baker Books
a division of Baker Publishing Group
PO Box 6287, Grand Rapids, MI 49516-6287
www.bakerbooks.com

Printed in the United States of America

Library of Congress Cataloging-in-Publication Control Number: 2020005176

ISBN 978-1-5409-0107-1

The author is represented by the literary agency of The Bindery, LLC.

20   21   22   23   24   25   26   7   6   5   4   3   2   1

*I would like to dedicate this book to Mom and Dad,
Lamar and Belinda Collier.
You saved my life.*

*And to my twin, Sara,
you gave me a life to fight for.*

CONTENTS

Contents

THE WORDS
THAT CHANGED
EVERYTHING

Every miracle is a reaction to the impossible. I would dare say that without the impossible, miracles would not be needed. Are you in need of a miracle? If so, I'm glad you're reading this book, because I was. My hope for you as we travel through what some would say is an inconceivable journey, which is my life, is that you would be inspired. Not only inspired but also filled with an unwavering hope that if God could do it for me, he can do it for you too. Here's my miracle story.

It was the fall of 2013 when my family and I found ourselves sitting inside a small studio within the thirty-seven-story NBC Tower in downtown Chicago, by way of Atlanta, Georgia. That was our first time in the Windy City. My twin sister, Sara, my father, Lamar, and my mother, Belinda, had traveled from Atlanta to be there, and now we were being taken through hair and makeup and ushered around by the senior producer, a woman named Dorothy. She seated Mom and Dad in the front row of the live studio audience and Sara and me on the couch right next to Steve Harvey—*the* Steve Harvey—the mogul, comedian, award-winning radio personality, producer, actor, author, and, most relevant to my story, television mega host. He was everywhere, doing everything it seemed, including humbly helping a pair of twenty-four-year-old twins find their birth mom. Or at least *trying* to help.

A year prior to this turn of events, we Colliers were sitting in the living room at the family house, watching a Falcons game, when Dad broke the only rule he'd ever given us in relation to watching football: *NO ONE TALKS* during the game. He waited quietly until a random fourth down and then hollered, "You know what you need to do?"

It wasn't a question.

We knew better than to holler back, even as our expressions communicated our shock. "You need to go find your parents!" Dad said, his voice still raised.

What you must understand about my father is that hollering was normal for him. I doubt he even knew he was doing it. In his head, he was speaking at a normal pitch, but to us? *Hollering*—no question. Still, we forgave him. He's from the part of the country where everyone shouts and thinks it's normal.

"What are you *talking* about?" I remember asking him.

As a family, the subject of "finding our birth mother" was new. Sara and I had never been interested or uninterested in

10

"finding" anyone or anything, because we'd never really felt that anything was lost.

"Well, you need to know where you came from," Dad said. "You're getting older. I think it may be time. I mean, you don't want to grow up and marry a cousin, do you? Because that could happen! You could marry your sister or brother, and you'd never know it!"

Sara and I both side-eyed him, chuckled, and thought, *So that's your argument, huh?*

Although we didn't admit it, Dad was right. My sister and I wouldn't have known our biological cousins or siblings if they were staring us in the face.

Dad then went on to holler, "And *another* thing. God told me *Steve Harvey* is going to help you do it! If he can't help you, no one can." It was in *that* moment I got up and left. "Dad," I said as I walked out the door, "I think you've lost your mind." I told my sister that she was in charge of this craziness and left.

. . .

"I'm sorry to tell you that nothing turned up," senior producer Dorothy had told my family. The show's producers had received Sara's letter a month prior, explaining that we'd been given up for adoption at birth and wanted to reunite with our biological mother and siblings, if we had any. "We know that if anyone can help us," she'd written, "it's Steve Harvey."

But evidently, even Steve Harvey has his limits. He had tried everything, we were told, but all roads led to a dead end. "Still," the producer had been kind and offered, "if you'd like to come on the show and make a plea to the nation to help you find your mother, we will pay your way here and back . . . you and your parents too. It would be a nice addition to our weeklong Mother's Day specials."

Figuring we had nothing to lose, we'd flown to Chicago and were sitting on the set, waiting, as an assistant cued the audience for applause to bring us in from a commercial break.

"Sam, let me ask you, what do you know about your birth mother?" Steve Harvey said.

The truth is, we didn't know much. As we prepared for the show, Mom unlocked the safe and pulled out our decades-old adoption paperwork, about one hundred pages of it that communicated the hard facts of our origin story—that we'd been born to a broken mother who, in her crossroads moment, decided that our best shot at life was the foster care system or adoption.

As I stood at a Kinko's copy center at two in the morning, photocopying those dozens upon dozens of pages to send to Steve Harvey's team, I gathered up the details of my mother's circumstances.

Legal Name: Elinor Lynette Redden
Age: 21
Residence: Augusta, Georgia
Marital Status: Single

There was evidence of welfare and extreme poverty. There were Child Protective Services reports and claims of prostitution. There were indications of the use of hard drugs—crack and cocaine among them. There were plentiful facts about our mother, but the news on our father was thin. The general consensus, as far as we could tell, was that he had completely deserted our bio-mom and was consistently strung out on drugs.

Nobody would have blamed me for holding on to rage for that man, but my posture toward him was warm. Was this because I had been raised by a loving dad? Maybe. But context has a way of providing clarity and creating empathy. Given the era my biological father grew up in, he was probably just doing what he had seen older men do. Like so many African-American men of his generation, he was a product of the social, economic, and environmental factors at work in the world around him. The prevailing emotion I felt as I read about him was something resembling pity.

What a terrible set of circumstances he had. What a frustrating way to live.

As I continued to read, I discovered that my bio-mom and bio-dad had had more kids before Sara and I came along. This unbelievable realization struck me under the copy center's fluorescent lights, as high-speed machines whirred and ground around me. I had a brother. I had two more sisters. This news struck me as *insane*. Three young kids. Three mouths to feed. And then, along came twins. Even a mature, emotionally stable woman could have buckled under the weight of that. For my mother, I imagined, it crushed her.

People who study drug addiction say that smoking crack consistently causes the user to experience a terrible mix of emotions, including irritability, anxiety, depression, aggression, and paranoid behavior. Yes, the highs are high, but the lows are equally low. So in addition to facing all the usual fears associated with being a young, poor, single mother, our mom probably dealt with at least some of those crippling effects. Sara and I consider ourselves blessed that we were given the gift of life in the first place. Many women who find themselves where our bio-mom found herself would have chosen abortion over adoption. Whatever her motivations, and whatever her reality, I like to believe that her decision to give us up had been based in love, even if it hadn't been. She let go of us and sent us upriver like the baby Moses in a basket, trusting that God would meet us, hoping that someone would find us, believing that somehow, some way, we'd be all right in the end.

· · ·

"The twins are looking for their birth mother," Steve Harvey was saying, "and their adoptive parents support this search. They're here, in fact. Lamar and Belinda, would you stand?"

The only mom and dad Sara and I have ever known stood up from their seats in the front row as the crowd around them erupted with applause. From the couch where we were sitting, we looked at them with pride. They were our heroes. Our rescuers. Our version of Jesus.

Out the corner of my eye, I took in my twin sister embodying all the beauty of a woman mixed with an uneasy smile in regard to who might enter the stage. If Sara was an actress, she could easily be cast as Serena Williams in an HBO movie special. My sister is a combination of academic smarts and physical fitness: she can float through complicated calculus problems as if she were playing tic-tac-toe, and focus on staying physically fit like an Olympic athlete. With espresso-brown skin and eyes that always warm my soul, Sara is simply breathtaking. That day she was sporting a short, curly, cropped hairstyle, which allowed her high cheekbones to command attention.

Looking at my mom in the audience, I knew the viewers would define her resting face as a genuine smile. A tall, slender, graceful woman, my mom could easily pass for a long-distance runner. Her caramel skin tone accentuates her compassionate eyes and intuitive nature.

I think my dad's honesty shows up in his face. His eyes tell a story of triumph through faithfulness. He could be described as having an average build, but his broad shoulders give him a soldier-like frame. Looking at him in the audience, I realized how all my life I had thought he could fix anything, solve any puzzle, stay calm through any crisis. I still believe that to be true.

My dad had been at every basketball game I'd ever played. All along the way, my mom made sure that Sara and I were given every educational opportunity any child could ever have. They'd introduced us to the living God—Jesus Christ himself. They'd loved us. And for the millionth time, there they were, laying aside their own agenda, to help Sara and me further God's plans for us. There Dad was again, being Dad. Standing at attention, living in the moment, clapping with the audience as Steve asked him and Mom to stand.

They deserve every moment of this applause and more, I thought to myself. *Man, my parents are the greatest.*

During that emotional moment, Steve Harvey looked at me and said, "Now I know I said that we didn't find your birth mother, but that's not the case."

He paused and then said the words that would change everything for Sara and me: "Elinor, come on out."

PART ONE

· · ·

YOU,
HERE AND
NOW

1

FAMILY MATTERS

I sustain myself with the love of family.

MAYA ANGELOU

"Family" doesn't always mean "blood." If you want to know one of the secrets to happiness in life, copy and paste that one onto your heart.

When I was a kid, my dad had a barbershop—Silver Star Barbershop. Still today, all these years after Dad left that business, Silver Star stands strong, one of the oldest businesses in the Sweet Auburn district, an area known primarily for being the birthplace of the Civil Rights Movement in Atlanta. Sweet Auburn is where Martin Luther King Jr.'s father pastored. Sweet Auburn is where Dr. King grew up. Sweet Auburn is where the historic Ebenezer Baptist Church and Dr. King's only organization, the Southern Christian

Leadership Conference, reside. My dad's Silver Star Barbershop was nestled between history. I didn't know any of this as a kid, you realize; to me, it was just "where Dad worked."

Most Saturday mornings, I'd be wakened from a deep, peaceful sleep by my dad hollering (of course), "Sam! Let's go! We gotta get down to the shop! Let's gooo!"

The truth was that I loved going down to the shop. What I didn't love was having an alarm clock that yelled.

In Dad's defense, my comatose state *required* a little hollering. From time to time, Dad would give up on trying to wake me and just leave me there to sleep. Around noon, I'd call him and ask why in the world he'd left me home. "Are you serious?" he'd say with a chuckle. Nuclear war couldn't have woken me up.

I'd hang up the phone and slink back to bed, determined not to miss his wake-up hollering the next time. That next time would come, and I'd heed the call. Father and son! Off to the Silver Star. Let's go, let's go, let's go.

Our journey to the shop always began with a quick stop at Chick-fil-A to get Dad's morning coffee and two chicken biscuits—one for him, one for me. It was followed up by the sounds of Kiss 104.1 FM, the oldies station, with the fly jock Tom Joyner and his crew trash-talking us onto I-20 East. We'd munch our biscuits to the I-75/85 North interchange, where the fog would clear and our exit would appear. Auburn Avenue—there it was. We were close, and I was glad.

I want you to think of the best of soul food dishes—whether it's collards, baked chicken, fried chicken, mac and cheese, banana pudding, or barbecue. Imagine the aroma of these dishes being personified into the warmest and most secure hug on a cold day. That feeling is Auburn Avenue. Walking outside the Silver Star Barbershop, you'd see Henry's Grill and Lounge directly across the street. It was an old-fashioned restaurant with a big cursive neon sign on top of the building. To the left of the barbershop was Poro Beauty Salon, where women entered wearing scarves covering their heads and exited with beautiful permed, teased, or silky straight hairstyles from the pressing comb. The Royal Peacock—a once-upscale nightclub boasting celebrity superstar performances by B.B. King, the Four Tops, and Atlanta's own Gladys Knight and the Pips—hosted reggae parties during my youth. A block up from the barbershop was the *Atlanta Daily World* newspaper, the first black-owned daily, and the African-American Panoramic Experience (APEX) Museum. At the corner of Auburn Ave and Piedmont Avenue was the beaux-style Atlanta Life Insurance Company complex. At the end of the block stood Big Bethel AME Church, or what I thought was a castle. The wide arches and a tower at the southern end, all covered with noble rough-hewn stones, gave the church a gothic feel. Perched on the top of the steeple was a white cross, and on the front as well as the back of the steeple were two blue neon cross signs with the words "Jesus Saves." To this day, driving on I-75/85 at night and seeing the bright neon "Jesus Saves" sign cutting through the darkness provides me comfort on many nights.

Auburn Ave (aka Sweet Auburn) was the mecca for black-owned businesses. Farther up Auburn Ave, past the I-75/85 bridge, was the historic Ebenezer Baptist Church where Rev. Dr. Martin Luther King Jr. became copastor with his father. Next door was the palatial Martin Luther King Jr. Center for Nonviolent Social Change, a memorial dedicated to Dr. King's legacy.

Riding with my dad every Saturday to the barbershop, I never thought to visit Ebenezer Church or the King Center. During holidays or the summertime, I would see lines of tourists eagerly waiting to take photos of the pulpit Dr. King preached from or to see his worn Bible or wristwatch displayed in the King Center. I imagined parents trying to put Dr. King's legacy in context for a young mind to grasp the magnitude of this freedom fighter. With all that history right up the street, I never thought to enter the space and take in the sites. I was a kid, and the thought of Dr. King's legacy seemed to be such an out-of-reach story for me to wrap my brain around.

Dad wasn't chatty on these trips. Keeping in line with his no-talking-during-football rule, these commutes were quiet. As a young boy who wanted nothing more than to be like his dad, I followed suit. Collier men were silent. I became silent too.

Filling in the space were area transit buses stopping and starting, homeless men shouting out their requests for cash, businessmen and Georgia State University students hustling and bustling through their morning routines. The city was *jumping*.

Eventually, we'd arrive, and Dad would tug out his key ring stuffed full with keys. He'd jiggle the lock, open the door, and walk laps around the shop as he got everything ready for the day.

Dad was always the first one to arrive, but shortly after, the rest of the Silver Star crew would come in. Black barbershops flow like a church service. Someone is always there to open the door and start the day, and between worship and the Word, everyone kind of trickles in. By the time the preacher gets up to preach, everyone is where they're supposed to be. In a black barbershop, the "preacher" is up by noon—ten a.m. on Saturdays. The culture of his "church" centers on what's always on TV in his shop, how good the coffee is, which customers are regulars, and what conversations are held.

If you ever witnessed the sheer madness of a black-barbershop debate, then you know that it's not for the faint of heart. You'd better come with *facts*. You'd better come with *passion*. You'd better come with *strength to go the distance*. I used to love being a fly on the wall whenever Dad's staff and clients went at it. In his unassuming way, Dad served as a quiet referee who secretly loved to indulge a few fools.

On one occasion, a Silver Star legend named Lucky started a debate about whether James Brown was the greatest recording artist of all time. This was the *king of soul* he was talking about. Things got crazy fast, mostly because everyone there forgot that Lucky's dad was once JB's bodyguard. "James Brown is the *king*!" half the shop (including Lucky) were hollering, while the others hollered, "James Brown is trash!"

Welcome to the black barbershop. Those fools were *family* to me.

As crazy and fun as the debates were, they were also empowering to me. I was a young man trying to sort out my identity, my character, my place in the world. To be allowed to be present for those discussions marked me. From time to time, someone would even ask my opinion on the debate at hand, and while the invitation made me sweat bullets, I loved feeling included like that. Those men weren't just customers or employees; they were big brothers and uncles and dads. They knew my name. They loved me and my dad. They cared about the progress I was making with every year that passed. Hanging around them told me much of what I needed to know about how to make it in this world. If it takes a village to raise a kid, well, these men were that village for me.

• • •

In this country, the term "family" historically has referred to a husband, a wife, and their biological offspring. Anything that doesn't run along those lines may be considered "family," but only if you throw some descriptive words before or behind it. If your mom isn't married, you're in a "single-parent family." If your mom or dad marries someone who has children of their own, you're part of a "blended family." If you're part of the LGBTQ community and have friends or partners who serve as your primary support system, you might be part of a "chosen family." If you've been adopted, like me, then you may refer to the individuals whose DNA runs through you as your "biological mother" or "biological father."

With that in mind, woven throughout contemporary science, sociologists and anthropologists have talked in terms of "degrees of kinship" when analyzing how people fit into and behave inside of family units. For example, the children of a parent are "first-degree" kin. Full biological siblings, half siblings, and biological grandmothers, grandfathers, nieces, nephews, aunts, and uncles are "second-degree" kin. Half nieces, half nephews, first cousins, and more are "third degree," whereas half first cousins are "fourth-degree," first cousins once removed are fifth, second cousins are sixth, and so on, right down the line. And with these degrees, we have great clarity. We have an answer to the question, "Who are you to me?"

Other than Sara, the lines weren't exactly clear regarding my connection to another human being. Which was cool with me, because we'd been loved, accepted, and welcomed by an *amazing* mom and dad. We may not have had a ton of external wealth, but *internal* riches? We had buckets and buckets of it. Sara and I are living proof that some of the poorest people in the world, materially speaking, are happier than some of the richest. Why? Because those "poor" ones have sorted out where true wealth really comes from. Kindness, patience, confidence, self-esteem, faith, integrity, love—these things were the glue that held our family together. Whatever "lack" I was supposed to be experiencing from the absence of my biological family, I just didn't have.

• • •

Researchers will tell you that the effects of "maternal abandonment" are almost always guaranteed to create substantial damage in the hearts and souls of its victims. There are evidently various forms that this type of abandonment can take, such as emotional maternal abandonment, where the mother is present with her children in body but miles away in her mind and heart. Or psychological maternal abandonment, where the mother regards her kids with hatred or apathy, often neglecting them and not tending to their basic needs. But these experts in the field agree that, by far, the worst form of maternal abandonment is the physical one, where the mom literally just leaves.

In the world of reptiles, abandonment is a part of their coming-of-age strategy. Snakes lay eggs filled with their babies, and even before those eggs hatch, the females exit stage left. Geckos do the very same thing.

To create a closer parallel, panda moms, who almost always deliver twins, keep one with them and abandon the other to the woods.

We read these facts and find ourselves resisting the urge to cringe: Aren't mothers hardwired to care for their young? We know there's something called *maternal instinct*, and regardless how fast and bright our independent streak runs, we still kind of expect moms to show up. This is why we just laugh when a baby starts to cry when his mother leaves the room. "Oh, it's okay," we say in a baby voice, an attempt to convince the child that his mother will be right back. Until a child experiences the development that occurs during the sensorimotor stage, the baby will always freak out. Why? Because until that point, I've learned, the baby believes that when an object disappears, it ceases to exist. If Mom leaves the room, Mom dies—which consequently makes the baby want to die too. "How will I live without Mama?"

But, of course, his mom hasn't ceased to exist. She's just using the restroom. All moms eventually come back. Right?

Back to the abandonment research: When a child is physically abandoned by the one who birthed him, in nearly every instance, chaos ensues. The child wonders what he did wrong to make his mother leave. The child may feel guilty—even though he's not sure what he's feeling guilty about. Later in life he may grow fearful of building relationships with other adults, because look what happened to the *first* adult he knew. He may walk through life expecting every person he is around to leave at some point. He longs for his long-awaited reunion with Mom. I mean, what other solution is there?

As I developed the ability to evaluate the world around me, to put words to that world and my life, to make sense of all that I'd been through, I saw that none of the expected results for someone like me had come to pass. In other words, I never felt abandoned, nor did I experience what the research communicates.

As far as I knew, our mother left and wasn't coming back, and that was a good thing for our future. I'd survived being abandoned by the woman who birthed me.

I'd survived two months of foster care—two months of Benadryl in my milk to keep me quiet because we were sickly and cared for poorly before the Colliers (Mom and Dad) showed up.

I'd even survived being rejected by couples filled with familial anticipation who might have adopted Sara and me but didn't because of the false prediction placed on my and Sara's life by the shortsighted, and dare I say racist, agency director. "You don't want *them*," she'd tell prospective adopting parents. "Because of where they come from, they probably won't amount to much."

Lately, whenever I speak to an audience or a congregation, I tell them that being from the black church, I need some energy in the room. To get the crowd warmed up, I ask them to turn to someone they don't know, smile, and say, "You look *good* today!"

Like the responsible, upstanding citizens they are, they follow suit, and the room quickly fills with encouragement and laughter as people receive a compliment that makes them feel good, even if it's not true. It's interesting to think back to my infant self and wonder if anyone back then had thought we looked good. I'm sure someone had to. I mean, look at me! Joke.

The truth is, our origin story attracted a dark cloud over us in that adoption home. That is, until Belinda and Lamar came by. "Oh, you don't want *them*," the director of the agency said. "Their mama was a druggie and a prostitute, and their daddy loved him some crack cocaine. These kids are for sure going to have *problems*. . . ."

That director believed that this was the truth of Sara and me and treated us according to that truth.

She'd leave me lying on one side of my head for weeks, causing my head to become misshapen over time. She'd put Benadryl, like I mentioned, in our bottles of formula. She never bent my sister's legs, leaving Sara frustrated and stiff. When Mom and Dad found us, we were a mess.

Still, they saw past all those barriers and blockages. "To be a mother to a child," musician Alicia Keys writes, "is the most brilliant gift."[1] Mom and Dad couldn't have kids of their own, so they decided that *we'd* be their kids; *we'd* be their gift. They didn't want just *any* babies to come home with them that day; they wanted *us*.

The abandoned ones.

The counted-out ones.

The left-for-dead ones.

The set-apart ones.

No matter the struggles, we'd be family—together, as one.

Even if you've been on this earth for just a short time, I'm sure you've come face-to-face with the feeling of being overlooked and dismissed. You work tirelessly, only to have someone else get the promotion. You put everything into a friendship, only to have the other person not hold up their end of the bargain—again. You pour out your heart to your significant other and get silence in return. You *invest*. And there's no return.

On the flip side, maybe you also know how it feels to be handpicked, chosen, called out from all the rest. Maybe you got picked for a playground game when you were a kid. Or you got chosen to be on student council. You were asked to go to a dance, accept a job, or become someone's husband or wife. Didn't you feel *seen*? In a world of seven billion people, to have someone look your way, take you in, and intentionally choose you is a special thing. For Sara and me, Mom and Dad's single act of selection, on a cold but hope-filled winter day, would mean the world. Four days before Christmas, Belinda and Lamar . . . Mom and Dad . . . stepped through the front door of their Georgia ranch-style home, a pair of car seats in their arms, and hollered as only Dad could, "We're here!"

Our future uncles and aunties, cousins, babysitters, and role models all lit up with eager anticipation as we stepped over the threshold and into the Collier universe. One of the matriarchs of the group leaned in to establish a familial bond and, in a voice barely above a whisper, said, "Everything is gonna be okay. You are one of us now."

One of us.

At last, we had a family. At last, we had a place to belong. We were part of an *us* now. We were no longer on our own.

How much did my infant mind know of this? Did my heart sense that something had changed? Essayist Diane Ackerman wrote that "[words] paint watercolors of perception."[2] I like to think that on the canvas that is my life, those words of love and acceptance—*you are one of us now*—established a soul-stirring portrait.

When I reexamine my place in the Collier family, the notion of adoption is woven throughout our lineage. Not only my family, but this notion of taking care of a child without a biological connection runs deep before and after the emancipation of the African slaves, reverberating those words, "You are one of us now." The establishment of adopting a motherless child because she was sold to another family or had escaped was a staple in the community. These familial relationships proved a powerful coping tool for slaves, especially those separated from blood relatives.

According to Pittsburg State University scholar Lucy Phelps Hamilton,

> The slaves took these relationships seriously and genuinely considered their fictive kin as blood family. This strategy allowed them to fill voids in one another's lives. While not biologically related, these women—the mothers, aunties, and grannies—loved "their" children and raised them as their

own. Through the adoption of motherless children, these women attained the respect and status of mothers within their community.[3]

I like to imagine how those slaves refused to allow the "abandoned baby" story to take hold of a motherless child left because the mother or father was auctioned or snatched by death. I like to imagine how those slaves walked the razor-thin boundary of bondage life daily and saw the greater story resting in an orphan child.

• • •

I look back now and find that while that day with Steve Harvey would go down as one of the most memorable experiences of my life—right up there with meeting Jesus and, later, meeting my wife—it didn't overwhelm me in the way that an outside observer might have expected it to. I didn't fall at Elinor's feet in a puddle of tears, crying, "Mom! Finally, the moment has come! It's you! It's *you*!"

I didn't experience that revelatory, identity-shaping, out-of-this-world feeling that long-awaited reunions can bring about. Unfortunately for the viewing audience, there was no "I'm finally whole! I'm finally complete!" moment. (Sorry, homies.)

No, meeting my biological mother didn't fill the monstrous hole left by her absence for the simple reason that there *was no hole*. I often say that if adoption is done in the right way, at the right time, by the right people, something special can happen. I'm not confident enough to guarantee this, but I am sure that adoption done right can fill holes

31

before they even truly form. So no, meeting my biological mother didn't fill a hole. But it did start something.

———• REFLECTION •———

So how'd your life start? Yeah, you—the one reading these words. Were you abandoned? What about accepted? Here's what I know. No matter how our lives started, by now we've all been accepted at some point by someone. Heck, even if that someone is only God. I'm not sure how difficult your beginning was—for some of you, I'm sure it was crazy, possibly even filled with massive abandonment and rejection. My hope for you is that, regardless of your circumstances and/or trauma, you will find a way to receive the acceptance that I guarantee is around you. Let yourself be accepted by someone who is dying to love you or by a God who already does.

2

CHURCH
CLOTHES

Darkness cannot drive out darkness; only light can do that.
Hate cannot drive out hate; only love can do that.

MARTIN LUTHER KING JR.

I grew up in a house where the Golden Rule ruled. Every major world religion has at its core some version of this idea of reciprocity, but for my parents, the Jesus version was the only version that mattered. In the Sermon on the Mount, after Jesus addresses some of the core topics that help shape the formation of our Christian ethic—anger, adultery, divorce, revenge, giving to the poor, prayer and fasting, money, possessions, and judging others—Jesus in effect says, "Look, if you don't want to have to remember the fine print on every issue, just do this: treat everyone the way you want to be treated—end of story." His exact words were: "Do to others whatever you would like them to do to you. This is the essence of all that is taught in the law and the prophets" (Matt. 7:12).

That was clear, easy to remember, and profound enough to be impactful in my dad's eyes. Plus, he agreed with it—simple as that. Anytime something in the Bible lined up with something that my father learned growing up in the country, he was game. For both my mom and my dad, if the Golden Rule was good enough for Jesus, then it was good enough for them. And for them, *good* was something they'd decided from the day they met would be their North Star. They had experienced enough *bad*.

Mom and Dad met on a Sunday. It was three o'clock in the afternoon when my mother walked into a laundromat near her home in urban Washington, DC. She was married at the time to her first husband, a wild man who was a part of the Black Panther Party, formed in the mid-1960s in Oakland, California, that prided itself on protecting the black community by any means necessary. This party formed at a time in history in which the black community was split between several strategies for resistance and preservation in a racist America. While Dr. King was teaching nonviolence, many others—including the Black Panther Party—were teaching retaliation. As the news media painted the organization as "hate spreaders," they often neglected to mention the Black Panthers' free breakfast programs in various cities. From 1969 through the early 1970s, the Black Panthers' Free Breakfast for School Children Program fed tens of thousands of hungry kids. However, my mom's first husband didn't gravitate to the organization's benevolent aspect. He was angry and directed his anger toward racist police, and Mom. A few hours before she headed for the laundromat, she decided she'd had enough.

My mom had already filed for divorce from her husband, but after the physical abuse encountered the night before, divorce seemed like a weak and dangerous option. She was young and scared, and in those days, "the law" wasn't exactly eager to rescue or protect endangered wives, especially poor, black ones. It seemed the safer solution would be to take matters into her own hands.

Over the years as Mom told me this story, the details only increased. By the time I was fourteen, she explained to me that the real reason she'd gone to the laundromat was to have an alibi. "An alibi?" I asked, incredulous. "What for?"

She said nothing in response, but the look in her eyes told me everything I needed to know. She felt justified for this plan, she explained to me, because the night before her trip to the laundromat, her husband had hit her in the head with a gun. Her options, as far as she could tell, were to kill or be killed.

But then a man happened into the same laundromat, and Mom's plan faded into thin air.

Lamar Collier also had his relational hands full. He was watching not his first, but his second marriage fall apart, and he was at the laundromat for a more straightforward reason: to wash his clothes. Life had been hard for him after his days in the Army—marriage, the birth of two boys who struggled at every stage, divorce, another marriage, the adoption of a daughter, another divorce underway. He wasn't sure what would relieve the pain he felt, but he was looking, searching, hoping for a way out.

His relief showed up in my mom.

The two had a rather friendly yet intriguing conversation. I'd be lying if I were to say that sparks didn't begin to fly. Especially after they both realized they were in the middle of a divorce. The conversation was respectful and light. It certainly wasn't enough to spark a relationship that day, but it was enough to distract my mom long enough from her troubles that she no longer felt compelled to carry out her violent plans. And to cause my dad to believe that a new day might, in fact, be dawning for him . . . that things could look up . . . that life could *work*.

They were married within a year.

• • •

My dad had grown up in Griffin, Georgia, the county seat of Spalding County, in the middle of nothing but plot after plot of farmland. There were more cows than people, and for most of the youth, the primary goal of life was just to get out. I'm not sure if Dad went to church much; he never really spoke about it. I assume he didn't. But given the size of his family—his mom and dad had twelve children—this makes sense to me. Probably to you too: Would *you* want to be responsible for getting a dozen kids bathed, dressed, and out the door if you didn't have to?

My dad's Aunt Mae was the midwife when he was born. She was the younger sister of my dad's dad (George Collier), and she lived to be 103 years old. Daddy and Aunt Mae were thick as thieves, and she doted on him. As the youngest

36

of a large family, half of his siblings were already married with families of their own during his childhood years. He was born after the fall of the stock market, and the Depression was easing off in the country, giving everyone a chance to catch their breath, but unemployment was lingering at 17 percent. My uncles and aunts describe my grandfather as a kind and gentle spirit who chose to discipline his kids with a serious talk rather than spanking. My dad lost his father when he was around five, which created a huge void in the Collier family.

When my dad was in high school, the household consisted of him, Sara Collier (my dad's mother), and two expectant sisters-in-law, Aunt Mamie and Aunt Lena. Back then, pregnant wives stayed with relatives to help take care of them while the husbands worked around the clock to prepare for the baby. My dad tells stories of how simple life was with only him and his mother. Every morning, he got enough water from the well, eggs from the chickens, and milk from the cows for the two of them. Once his sisters-in-law moved in, his workload doubled. After the birth of his nephew (Jeffery), my dad and his mom were the primary caregivers for a few years because the baby's parents were working constantly to provide a comfortable life. The three amigos— Dad, his mother, and Jeffery—spent their days fishing in the Flint River, riding around town, and sometimes just looking up at the starry night.

To say my dad loves his siblings would be an understatement. As the youngest, he was always ready to jump in and help out whenever needed. Running parallel was my dad's faith in God's protection. This faith was put to the test in

August of 1992 when Hurricane Andrew hit Miami. Homestead in Dade County was the home of my three aunts (Aunt Hattie Mae, Aunt Louise, and Aunt Christine) and two uncles (Uncle Leon and Uncle Milton, aka Uncle Po Boy). Five of my dad's siblings were in the direct path of that Category 5 hurricane. He and two of my uncles (Uncle John in Atlanta and Uncle Marvin in Los Angeles) wrestled with the urge to hit Miami like the cavalry and bring their family to higher ground. As the story goes, my dad and his two brothers had to sit by the phone, waiting to hear from their siblings. Looking back on that white-knuckled time, my dad bounced between bargaining with God to protect the family he loved in Miami and finally owning Psalm 46:10—"Be still, and know that I am God!"

Sara and I, at four years old, were unaware of the anxiety my parents were experiencing, but we felt something was different. My parents tried to maintain an *everything is fine* attitude, but a low-level panic punctuated their movements.

It was Monday night, which meant Monday night football so my dad's "No talking during football" rule was in effect. That night, the TV was not blasting the game. It was quiet in the house, except for my parents on the phone, trying to contact our Miami family.

The news reporters described a nuclear-disaster type of devastation in Florida. Hurricane Andrew stripped homes down to the concrete foundations with wind speeds as high as 165 miles per hour. Neighborhoods populated with community centers, churches, and department stores were flattened, resembling a barren desert. Busy phone circuits became unbearable for my parents as they watched photos of the wreckage on the news, looking hard to find our family standing behind a newscaster. Finally, a cousin was able to get through on the phone and report that all the Florida Colliers were safe physically, but their homes were destroyed. My dad traveled to Miami to help his siblings, and the reality of the destruction came when he could not find the street his sister lived on. He said nothing in the vicinity resembled a residential area—it looked more like a developing country. The rebuilding was slow, but the Collier family had to dig deep and bond together to support each other. According to the National Weather Service, Hurricane Andrew destroyed more than 63,500 houses, damaged more than 124,000 others, caused $27.3 billion in damage, and left 65 people dead.

Mom's family was a bit smaller than Dad's. She is the oldest of two brothers and one sister, and she grew up in our nation's capital, which was a hotbed of political activity. During Mom's formative years, the murder of Emmett Till, a fourteen-year-old African-American who was lynched in Mississippi, was a defining moment for her. This act of violence sparked Mom's activist spirit at an early age. The Civil Rights Act of 1957, Greensboro sit-ins, and the Montgomery bus boycott fueled by Rosa Parks forced Mom to take an active role in the fight for freedom and equity. However, against the backdrop of her social activism, music fed her soul on different levels. Acoustic musicians such as Simon and Garfunkel, Bob Dylan, Woody Guthrie, and Joan Baez singing protest songs birthed out of American folk music energized and exposed her to labor and global politics. Of course, the music of Motown, including the Supremes, the

Miracles, the Temptations, the Four Tops, Martha and the Vandellas, and Marvin Gaye, spoke to Mom's very life of heartache, joy, and teenage angst.

Mom was only fourteen years old during the iconic March on Washington for Jobs and Freedom. This was the event that gave us Dr. King's "I Have a Dream" speech.

Mom made the bold decision to attend Howard University, a notable, historically black college. This is the university that educated Thurgood Marshall, first African-American United States Supreme Court Justice; Toni Morrison, Nobel Prize for Literature recipient; Richard Smallwood, Grammy Award–winning gospel singer; Roberta Flack, Grammy Award–winning singer; Ralph Bunche, Nobel Peace Prize recipient; and so many others. It seems that Howard University's motto, "Truth and Service," made an indelible mark on my mom. The ideology of "truth" gave birth to my mom's quest for "truth of self" or her authentic self. Decades later, this quest led Mom (with Dad beside her) to the teachings of the Faith Healing Clinic in Washington, DC.

When my parents met while living in Washington, DC, they were ready to embrace their greater story. By the time Dad was a grown man, what he had to show for himself was a rather cool demeanor and quiet confidence, two failed marriages, one son suffering with HIV/AIDS, another son stuck in prison for who knew how long, and a lonely yet warm heart. When one of Dad's brothers, Uncle John, became a pastor, Dad's interest was piqued. For the first time in his life, he started going to church near our home.

For some people—maybe you as well—"surrendering to Jesus" is a slow and sporadic transition where they lean in one iteration at a time, with every iteration getting a little more rocky, emotional, intriguing, and scary. It's not that they aren't sincere in their decision to follow Jesus; it's just that turning over control to an "invisible force" can freak a person out. My parents are the *other* kind of people, the kind who jump in with both feet while smiling. Like the first disciples Jesus called—Simon Peter, Andrew, James, and John, who upon encountering Jesus "immediately followed him" (Matt. 4:18–22), leaving behind their boats and their families alike—Mom and Dad knew a good thing when they saw it, and to them, Jesus was very good.

In the African-American community, we may not all start out loving Jesus, but when it's time to "come home" for one reason or another, we all seem to make our way there. Usually through a series of events that often include hitting rock bottom because of our own decisions, we come home. While neither my mom nor my dad had any real use for Christianity before, they were fully devoted believers from that point onward. They talked the talk. They walked the walk. They encouraged and, many times, dragged Sara and me to our church in Georgia on Sundays. They were *in* this way of living. They were in it for good.

Dad was eventually so transformed by the life-changing power of God that he became a preacher of God's Word. Dad looked up to his brother John and had followed in his footsteps now twice: once when he took over the barbershop on Auburn that John used to run, and a second time as he took over Uncle John's church. Practically, this meant that my family went from attending a kid-friendly, ten-thousand-member multicultural church to a small, backwoods community that boasted twenty people on Easter. In no time, we were running the place. We arrived early. We stayed late. Dad did his best to serve those twenty well.

At that time I was already interested in music, and my father promised me that if I would agree to help out with the music on Sundays, he would buy me the Triton, which was a massive, full-size, weighted keyboard by Korg. If you were a serious producer, you had one. The *Triton*. It was the greatest of all production modules during that time, and even at age twelve, I knew I needed one. I wanted to be as strong a producer as Pharrell Williams and as distinctive a performer as Usher. Well, a *Christian version* of Usher. Dad knew that holding out the Triton like a carrot would lock me in musically with New Hope Baptist.

Every Sunday morning I woke to the smell of Jimmy Dean sausage. I stumbled out of bed and wandered toward my seat at the kitchen table, where I inhaled a plate of eggs, bacon, sausage, and grits as the king of the black church, Bishop T. D. Jakes, wailed from the enormous old-school TV perched on the living room floor. After breakfast, Dad and I carried the weighty Triton through the house and down the porch toward the back of our beloved white Volvo station wagon. That car was a box on wheels, but it was *our* box.

Only after strategically loading in the Triton were humans allowed to wedge themselves in too. Mom and Sara slipped into their assigned seats, being sure not to bonk their heads on the unforgiving corners of the keyboard, and off we'd go. I-20 East, exit University Avenue, two right-hand turns, and there we were in the hood, home to New Hope Baptist Church.

I need to paint you a picture of the hood of the church. It was in an area of Atlanta known as Pittsburgh. Back in the day, the area was described as a working-class, black community with self-reliant and proud residents. Starting in the 1960s, the neighborhood began a slow decline as black families relocated to previously all-white areas. By the 80s, the slow decline accelerated into a rapid downward spiral as home values depreciated.

Trust me, I've heard stories about New Hope's celebrated years. My Uncle John organized the church months after Dr. King was assassinated. As a Civil Rights worker, he longed for a new brand of hope after riots threatened to tear this country apart. When climbing the steps up to the church became more challenging, Uncle John saw my dad as the next leader of his flock.

When I started attending New Hope, the neighborhood was peppered with abandoned homes, vacant lots filled with broken cars, and small, high-priced convenience stores that replaced the larger chain grocery stores. I remember seeing lines of cars parked on the streets because none of the homes had driveways. This was a depressed area, but the few members of New Hope were determined to show men to God and God to men. Me? I just wanted to play the Triton.

I quietly played the keys—"mood music"—as people arrived. I played as Dad put on his preaching robe. I played all throughout the service, rising in volume as Dad hit his three key points with passion—points that always emphasized faith. I played and played and played songs about Jesus, despite the R&B chords in my head. Bless New Hope's heart for indulging my version of "Amazing Grace," which sounded like a Stevie Wonder hip-hop remix. They were determined to support a young man's attempt to "get" gospel someday.

While I never did "get" gospel music, through my dad's solid teaching, I got the message.

Sitting there Sunday after Sunday, I couldn't help but take in exhortations to be respectful, to keep my feet planted on the path of righteousness, and to practice things like patience and goodness and love. I remember my father bringing homeless people from Auburn Avenue home to cut the grass and earn some income, saying, "Get the man a glass of cool water, Sam." I was confused at the time about why these homeless people were in our yard, but over time I saw that it was just kindness at work. He was treating them like he'd want to be treated. There was that Golden Rule at work.

Dad preached what he lived: Be noble. Be truthful. Be kind. Be the best version of you that you can possibly be.

Bring *all of you* to this great, big world.

Even though I played the required church music, the gospel song that cut straight through to my soul and set my musical lexicon ablaze was "Brighter Day" by Kirk Franklin. If you have not heard that song, please put this book down, find the song, listen, then pick this book back up. The song opens with a wicked guitar intro—similar to a Funkadelic throwback—and then Kirk Franklin hits the mic, telling us to "come get your bounce on" while the horns pump out hard over the funky guitar intro! I still get charged thinking about it. That song opened my eyes to the wider world of gospel music, and I was hooked. My blood already pumped music 24/7, but this new urban gospel grabbed me and would not let go. And when I thought about how the word *gospel* means the Good News and how traditional gospel music evolved, I could not help but gravitate to its great story even more.

Allow me to unpack my meaning. When I dove into the origins of gospel music during American slavery, I could feel the heartbeat melodies and low earth hums that wrapped around the sharp musical chords to give birth to the spirituals. Stepping further into this story, I listened to Harriet Tubman's hidden messages cloaked in the spirituals—such as "Go Down, Moses" to signify that a "deliverer" was nearby—and I stood in amazement. Scanning this story even deeper, I came across Thomas Dorsey, the father of gospel music and my homeboy (he was from Villa Rica, Georgia). He stepped into his musical talent, first through down-home blues as a composer for blues megastars Ma Rainey and Bessie Smith. Understand, that was happening around the 1920s and 30s, and Mr. Dorsey walked away from secular music (a lucrative career) to gospel music. He married the blues styles and rhythms with religious lyrics, which electrified the listeners. Building onto the gospel music story, the gospel quartets started a new direction around the 40s. Groups such as the Dixie Hummingbirds, the Soul Stirrers, and the Five Blind Boys of Mississippi built on Mr. Dorsey's work.

Looking back over the gospel music story, with each decade building upon the narrative, I have to give thanks to the legacy that produced the thumping beat I was nodding my head and patting to—Mr. Franklin's "Brighter Day." At fourteen years old, my musically inclined friends and I found our sacred place in this music. Don't get me wrong. We were still jamming to Usher's "You Don't Have to Call," J.Lo's "All I

Have," and Missy Elliot's "Work It"—but "Brighter Day" spoke a musical language that I understood wholeheartedly.

At New Hope, the congregation allowed my group and me to perform "Brighter Day" during the church service. We rehearsed the song countless times until we perfected it masterfully. I discovered how rehearsing prepared me to perform the song, but it did not prepare me for the audience's response. I had anxiety wondering how my traditional church home would receive this urban gospel song. Their staples were songs like "Just a Closer Walk with Thee," "Jacob's Ladder," and "Jesus Is All the World to Me." Keep in mind, this was an older congregation who was raised with and loved the spirituals. Would they reject my view of gospel music? So many gospel singers were criticized for melding secular and sacred music; would that be my same fate? I had to shake off those negative thoughts and step up to the plate. I had to realize how fear was trying to stifle me and, instead, press forward. I had to realize that God was in charge and my intention was to spread the Good News through song.

Standing behind the pulpit, where my dad would deliver the sermon, I started the first chords of "Brighter Day." My Uncle John gave a shout in support, but he was the kind of man who loved any type of music. My parents were clapping in time, but they were my parents—they're supposed to support me, right? Then, the older deacons started clapping in time, which spread to the congregation. A woman from the Mother's Board, dressed in white with a signature hat, jumped up and shouted out, "*You better sing, boy!*" Shouts reverberated throughout the small church mixed in with tears of joy over Kirk Franklin's lyrics, reminding us of the overwhelming love Jesus has for us. Overwhelming love. A love so massive, so uncomplicated, so intense that it confounded my heart in the most beautiful way. The older church members gave real, earthshaking testimonies of how Jesus pulled them through rough times to an unimaginable brighter day. Where the song left off, they picked up with their greater story. Immersed in that feeling, I thought my heart would burst. From that day, I tried to replicate the energy of "Brighter Day" through my rudimentary compositions. I wasn't ready to compose yet. I needed a teacher to guide me and add to my story.

• • •

Recently, I was thinking about what it was like to grow up in Atlanta, the mecca of black culture, in the 1980s and 90s. In addition to drilling into my heart and my head that Sara and I were not *less than* for being adopted, but rather *special* and *chosen*, Dad also taught us that our blackness was not a liability but an asset, not something to despise but something to treasure. That being black was about being born great.

I grew up black. Black neighborhood. Black music. Black people. Those black people taught me what it means to truly live. Being black means having a strong community. Being black means knowing how to *eat*. Being black means overcoming the struggles that attempt to limit you. Being black means striving for *excellence* in everything.

This wasn't how it always had been for people of color, of course. We came to this country as slaves. The inhumane treatment of our people sparked the Civil War. We endured Reconstruction and its crippling effects, and we fought until we finally could live as free people. Until we could be considered citizens of this country we called home, until we could vote in this country, until we could be educated properly, until we could eat at a white man's café and drink from a white man's water fountain.

Eventually, a black person would file a patent.

Eventually, a black person would become the bishop of a church.

Eventually, a black person would head a major political party.

Eventually, black people would be allowed to own banks, serve as foreign ministers, play on a "white" college's football team, perform at Carnegie Hall, publish a newspaper, receive a PhD from an Ivy League school, significantly influence agricultural practices, play professional golf, teach black *and* white students, become recording artists, write a book with a "big" publishing house, found a fraternity, star in a major motion picture, warrant equal protection by a jury, write a Broadway play, form a basketball team, write and publish church music, run track competitively, compete as heavyweight boxers, receive higher-education scholarships and grants, receive an Academy Award, receive an award for bravery in battle, become a general in the United States Army, serve in the United States Congress, host a radio variety show, become the president of a university, play Major League Baseball, win an Olympic gold medal, work as a professor at an esteemed medical school, join the National Basketball Association and the National Football League, become a rock-and-roll star, perform with the New York Metropolitan Opera, found a record company, win a Grammy, win

48

the Heisman, win a NASCAR race, pilot a spy plane, own a car dealership, serve on the United States Supreme Court, play professional tennis, win a Pulitzer Prize, cover a major fashion magazine, run for president, fly a commercial plane, win a Nobel Prize, start a TV station, become Miss America, be named US Poet Laureate, become an astronaut, and serve as CEO for a billion-dollar corporation.

After my sister and I came on the scene in 1988, the possibilities of black people seemed endless; from that day until this one, a black person has gone on to become the United States Surgeon General, the president of the American Medical Association, and the president of the American Association of Retired Persons.

Michael Jordan blew up the game of basketball, and Tiger Woods revolutionized the game of golf. Black women and men have served as mayors of some of the largest, most influential cities in our country. Both Condoleezza Rice and Colin Powell became secretary of state. Barack Obama became president. Oprah, Serena, and Beyoncé *still* kill it in their respective fields.

And while these steps of progress, and a thousand more that I didn't mention here, are cause for celebration, not one of them came without a *battle*, without plenty of people fighting us, telling us to sit down and shut up. There were death threats, bombings, beheadings. There were lynchings. Astoundingly, in 1952, the Tuskegee Institute reported that in its seventy-one-year history of operations, that year had been the first year without a single lynching reported. When you're different, life is different, and historically for black people, things have been different here.

Many have opinions about how black people should have handled the march toward progress more peacefully, with greater grace. I respect that; we live in a free country. But the fact is, when an entire group of people are marginalized, separated, beaten, and killed for requesting basic human rights, those people tend to get *tired*. They get worn down. They get sick and tired of being—you know the rest—sick and tired. They want a better life for themselves.

And so, amongst the weariness, that group at some point must choose to reach for better. I mean, isn't that what Jesus did? Didn't Jesus reach for better?

That group might start to band together and *demand* the rights they seek. They might appear a little . . . insubordinate.

They might seem unwilling to back down, maybe harsh.

They might resort to saying and doing things nice people don't typically choose to say or do.

And they might keep at it until things change.

But here's the thing: Even when things *do* change, as was the case with the Civil Rights Movement of the 1950s and 60s, those things aren't all the way "better" right away. Educational inequalities still existed. Real estate redlines were still drawn. Workplace discrimination was still a very real thing. Access to credit was still awfully tight. Household-income stats were still wildly out of balance: The *Washington Post* states that between 2013 and 2016, the wealth gap between black and white families grew by 16 percent, and by 14 percent between Hispanics and whites. In 2016, white families had a median net worth of $171,000, compared with $17,600 for blacks and $20,700 for Hispanics.[1]

Let's not even talk about incarceration rate disparities between white and black men that have *always* existed. So you start to see how things could go south. Single black moms have always done their best to parent their children while also maintaining two or three jobs, but all the effort in the world wouldn't have been enough to protect their daughters and sons from the darkness marking our culture in that current moment.

The drug epidemic. Alcohol. Gang violence. Crime. The hypersexualization of music and movies. Many of these influences impacted our heritage.

When my sister and I started learning the truth of where we came from, we learned that while we shared the same mother and father with our biological siblings, those biological parents had not been exclusive sexually. They had never married and, from the looks of things, had never enjoyed mutual respect. Our mother had begun having children at sixteen years of age. Both she and our father were heavy drug users. Neither of them had a steady income, which was perhaps what drove them toward dealing drugs and engaging in prostitution. My biological grandfather died in prison while serving two life sentences for committing a double homicide; several of my biological uncles are still doing time for dealing; and if not for my biological mother, Elinor, passionately insisting that my brother be shielded from the streets, he probably would have followed suit. In fact, to this day, my brother and I are the only men in our entire lineage not on drugs, in jail, or dead.

The parents who raised me, Belinda and Lamar, didn't come to their marriage squeaky clean either, as I've mentioned.

They had tasted and seen the effects of the dark side of black culture enough to know that they wanted something different for their kids. And so they vowed that if they got nothing else right, they'd at least protect us. They'd care for us. They'd keep us from becoming a statistic like so many kids our age.

• • •

That "protection" Mom and Dad sought came initially by osmosis. Every Saturday morning as Dad and I headed from our house to Silver Star, we drove past the thirty-five-acre Martin Luther King Jr. National Historical Park, site of MLK's childhood home; the church where he preached, Ebenezer Baptist Church; and a tribute to Civil Rights activists from all over the world, the International Civil Rights Walk of Fame. I could vividly see the eternal flame that burned brightly on the King Center grounds. The prolific words carved into the rock surrounding the flame—"The Dream Lives, The Legacy Continues"—hovered above me throughout my childhood like an angel keeping watch. I didn't understand the gravity of those words until I was much older, but I did know that they were important. That they were weighty. That they were supposed to matter to me. Behind the scenes of my young life, God was inviting me to protect and preserve Dr. King's good work.

A few blocks from there, I could see Morehouse, Clark, and Spelman Colleges—the Atlanta University Center— where so many black kids were pursuing excellence. The mere presence of those campuses called me to also do something worthwhile with my life, to believe that I could actually make a difference in this world.

I'd turn on the TV and see black teens with a platform wrestling with the issues of the day on Black Entertainment Television's "Teen Summit"—and I'd be encouraged to speak up for those who couldn't speak up for themselves too.

I remember going to school during Black History Month, which is in February, and being empowered by those in authority to *shoot for the stars*. To *work smarter*. To *do better* than everyone else, including those who are not black. Average was not enough, not if we kids wanted to overcome the obstacles we faced. The intercom would ring on, and we would be asked to join hands to belt out Rosamond and James Weldon Johnson's beloved black national anthem, "Lift Every Voice and Sing." We'd raise our voices to sing their words: "Sing a song full of faith that the dark past has taught us; Sing a song full of the hope that the present has brought us." As kids, we had no idea what we were singing. All we knew was that those lyrics had been birthed during a time of oppression, that we were no longer living in that type of oppression, and that we'd still better do our best to make our ancestors proud. We read about Rosa Parks and Jackie Robinson. We watched Michael Jordan make history on the basketball court. We were washed by Maya Angelou's poetic prowess. We looked at pictures of Harry Belafonte and wondered how a black man could be so fly. Through these and a thousand more examples, my friends and I were called to a level of intellectual, athletic, and musical greatness that we just assumed was part of being black.

Years later, on Auburn Ave, I noticed a vibrant mural of Representative John Lewis, part of Atlanta's Civil Rights royalty, and I smiled. This was the same John Lewis who posed for a picture with me when I was just six years old, just another customer in Dad's barber chair. I stared at that three-story mural and thought, *Being black is beautiful*. The bar had been set, and that bar was up high. I was to strive. I was to succeed. I was to soar. What I *wasn't* to do was precisely what I ended up doing: settle for anything less than that.

• • •

In 1998, a Pulitzer Prize–winning columnist named William Raspberry visited Morehouse College and stood before an audience filled with social advocates, activists, and strong thinkers on the subjects of cultural norms and cultural change who had flown into Atlanta from all over the country for a conference about African-American fathers—and Raspberry opened the first keynote session by saying, "Are black fathers necessary? You know, I'm old and I'm tired, and there are some things that I just don't want to debate anymore. One of them is whether African-American children need fathers. Another is whether marriage matters. Does marriage matter? You bet it does. Are black fathers necessary? D**n straight they are."[2]

I was ten years old at the time and had no idea who Mr. Raspberry was, that this conference was going on, or how the absence of a father could possibly affect my life. But affect it, it would, and in a swift three years' time.

A report titled "Turning the Corner on Father Absence in Black America" stated, "Of all Black babies born in 1996 [by way of example], approximately 70 percent were born to unmarried mothers." Further, the researchers behind the report explained that "on average a Black child born in the early

1950s would eventually spend about four years (or about 22 percent of childhood) living in a one-parent home. But for Black children born in the early 1980s, that figure . . . would nearly triple, to almost 11 years or about 60 percent of childhood."[3]

Some people say that this tumor within the black community increased because of the crack epidemic, which dominated the inner city in the 1980s. Some say it's because of pregnancies outside of the confines of marriage and the rapid growth of the divorce rate. Some say it's because of the rise of hip-hop. Any way you sliced the stats, everyone agreed that this was a *problem*.

The challenge with living in a post-Christian society is that while we can flaunt the freedoms we enjoy—to live how we want, to have sex with whomever we want, to have babies whenever and however we want—we can't escape the consequences those *freedoms* always bring. "Children who grow up in a household with only one biological parent are worse off, on average, than children who grow up in a household with both of their biological parents," the report continued, "regardless of the parents' race or educational background, regardless of whether the parents are married when the child is born, and regardless of whether the resident parent remarries."[4]

Children who live apart from their fathers are five times as likely to be poor. Girls who live apart from their fathers are *seven* times as likely to become pregnant as a teen. Children who live apart from their fathers face double the risk of infant mortality, of childhood obesity, and of dropping out of high school. They are more likely to have behavioral problems, more likely to face abuse and neglect, more likely to abuse drugs and alcohol, more likely to go to prison, and more likely to commit a crime.[5]

By creating a loving and stable marriage, my parents had done all they could do to set up Sara and me for success. They'd done all they could do to shield us from the emotional and psychological trauma we were destined to encounter had we stayed with our biological family. What they *couldn't* control were the families living right down the street from us—the families Sara and I would hang with after school and on the bus to school, the PTA moms, the hyperfocused sports dads coaching the peewee leagues. Those families were *different*. And those families' circumstances were *very, very* different from ours. Unfortunately for me, that difference was not a good thing. When "everyone" is thinking one way, it's hard not to think those same thoughts. I call it the power of collective thought. When "everyone" is saying one thing, it's hard not to say those same words. When "everyone" is doing one thing, it's hard not to do that thing. My public-elementary-school circle was filled with friends who were fatherless, either because their dads were never in the picture to begin with or because their parents had divorced. It's worth noting that in the 144 years that researchers have been studying marriage and divorce rates in this country, the *highest rate* of divorce occurred between 1980 and 1993—my preteen years.[6]

All in all, my life began to take a turn. The negative influences my parents had worked so hard to protect me from had found a way to me. Call it peer pressure, the desire to fit in, or just plain ole proximity. Emotionally, I had *left home.*

The question that remained was whether I'd ever find my way back.

------- • **REFLECTION** • -------

What statistics have you been able to circumvent, and which ones do you feel you may be slowly becoming? How'd you circumvent them? What has been the driving force that opened a door to the statistics you may now find yourself living in?

Friends, your ability to overcome or succumb doesn't change God's ability to turn your current mess into a message. Be encouraged that you are not alone in your quest as you grow and strive for better.

3

THE DAY MY
LIFE BECAME
MY OWN

*It's fine to celebrate success, but it is more
important to heed the lessons of failure.*

BILL GATES

If you had asked me back when I was a kid what I really wanted to be when I grew up, I would've said Michael Jordan. Every night, even when it was raining outside, I stood in the driveway of our house in Decatur and shot one hundred times into the portable basketball hoop I made Dad buy. (If you didn't have the basketball goal, were you really even serious?)

A hundred shots a night—that was the deal. I couldn't go to bed until I hit one hundred. In my heart, I knew I was destined to go pro. This was the blind optimism the Atlanta black community instilled in you. "Anything is possible if you believe!"

I *believed*.

Even though the "Be Like Mike" Gatorade commercials were in the past, I was still striving to *be like Mike* in 2001 at thirteen years old. After a short retirement, Michael Jordan returned to the NBA, and I had to get my game on by watching the master. According to ESPN, Jordan donated his first year's salary to relief agencies working with the victims of September 11.[1] What a philanthropist and GOAT (Greatest of All Time)! I was team MJ all the way. His signature dunk, his tongue hanging out each time he drove the ball to the basket, was insane! Floating through the air from the free throw line to the basket with his arms looking more like wings—I tried to mimic his every move.

What I should have done was *look in the mirror*. I was short. Really short. But because I *believed*, I figured that didn't matter. If I stretched my arms enough, I would grow. Surely, I'd grow. My mom believed with me. So we would stretch our arms together. (Thanks, Mom.)

I made only about half of those nightly shots, but because I *believed*, I figured that didn't matter, that it was okay. If I kept at it, I would get better. Surely, I'd get better.

To add insult to injury, I didn't have the right basketball shoes, the shoes that Rosby's grandma got him. But because I *believed*, I figured that didn't matter. Once I went pro, I'd be able to afford the right shoes. (Which perhaps explains my humble obsession with vintage Jordans today.) Surely I'd make it in the big leagues.

I had the belief. Added to that, I had the *potential* for height, accuracy, and swag. Now I just needed a team. Until then, Mom had Sara and me enrolled in magnet schools, which was great if you wanted to be a doctor. Not so great if you wanted to go pro in the NBA. So I launched a master plan to start attending Columbia Middle School, a new school in town that I believed would be the perfect bridge from AAU sports to high school ball. The magnet school I attended, Snapfinger Elementary, went through the seventh grade, and high school began at grade nine. My grand plan was to attend Columbia for eighth grade and play basketball for them. It was also true that Columbia Middle let their seventh and eighth graders march in the band. I was already marching with my alto saxophone, so I figured basketball was next!

Mom had a different plan.

One day during my seventh-grade year, Mom picked me up from choir practice and proceeded to drive off in the opposite direction of home. "Mom, where are we going?"

Without taking her eyes off the road, she smiled and said, "I'm taking you to your *audition*."

"Wait, what? What audition?"

She then told me that she had set up an audition for me at the only high school performing arts conservatory in town. This was the audition that kids prepared for for *years*. Ever seen the movie *Fame*? This was the Dirty South's version of *Fame*.

I shouldn't have been surprised by my mom's actions that day. She was forever doing whatever it took to ensure a proper future for Sara and me. For example, when my sister and I were in the third grade, Mom quit her well-paying corporate FedEx job to be a secretary in the school system. Her reasoning behind this was simple: Go where the action is! Uncover the opportunities that fly under the radar! Give those little black kids of hers a leg up!

Well, Mom's plan had worked. The week prior to that drive from school, my mother had found a notice on the faculty bulletin board that announced upcoming auditions for artistically talented students. You remember my musical Usher ambitions I mentioned earlier? Well, this was the beginning of those aspirations. Somewhere along the way, singing along with Usher on the radio while participating in choir had led some girls in my class to tell me I could sing. So while Sara had straight As since kindergarten, I had . . . other . . . gifts. I still believed that basketball was one of them, but Mom didn't exactly agree anymore. She wanted to know that whatever Sara and I were invested in today would make for a profitable future tomorrow; according to her, basketball wasn't part of that plan. I needed to grow, and that just wasn't happening. I needed to pursue a different dream.

For years my parents, my sister, and all our extended family told me that I was going to be the next superstar. "You're gonna make it big, Sam!" they'd cheer at the family reunion banquets. "You'll be the family's first millionaire!"

I did love music. And my voice wasn't half bad. But did I really have what it took?

It is said that one of the jobs of a good parent is to forecast the future for their child based on that kid's talents and gifts and to then guide the child in the right direction so that his or her potential can be drawn out. Mom was *good* at that job. I believe she noticed my long-awaited growth spurt just wasn't meant to be. I believe she noticed that music came naturally for me. I believe she knew I needed help shaping my dreams. I believe she was *determined* to give me the best life I could have.

The audition, I discovered there in Mom's car, was off North Druid Hills at DeKalb School of the Arts (DSA), a performing arts high school for grades eight through twelve. "Mom, these kids have been rehearsing for years. I literally have nothing to audition with," I explained.

But she just said, "Just sing whatever you were rehearsing when I picked you up. And play your saxophone. Everything will be fine once you start playing your saxophone." And when I told her that I didn't have my saxophone with me, she said, "It's in the back."

We pulled up to DSA, and the place was crawling with kids. Kids in leotards practicing their routines. Kids with every instrument under the sun warming up with scales. Kids singing their hearts out as though their future rested solely on one song. When it was finally my turn to audition, I stood in line and waited for my name to be called. The dancer who auditioned just before me exited the audition chambers, and I knew it was my time. I calmly walked to the front of the room. There was no way I was getting into this school, so I figured I'd just have some fun.

"Whenever you're ready," one of the judges said.

I played a little "Swing Low, Sweet Chariot" on the sax and then unfolded the choir lyrics that were stuck in my pocket from rehearsal. I started singing the lyrics to Bill Withers's 1972 classic "Lean on Me."

When I got to the chorus, I was feeling it. "Lean on me," I belted out, "when you're not strong. And I'll be your friend, I'll help you carry on . . ."

It was *good*.

But was it *DeKalb School of the Arts* good? Based on the wild talent tucked in every nook and cranny of the school that day, I knew the answer was no.

There. Are you happy, Mom? I did the audition. I won't be going to that school. Can we talk about basketball now?

Two months later, my parents, Sara, and I were at a restaurant having dinner when Mom whipped an envelope from her purse. "Saaam," she sang, "look what came in the mail today!"

The return address was DSA. "Mom, I *told* you. I am *not* going to that school!"

"Look," Mom said, "you don't have to go if you really don't want to, but let's at least see what it says."

We opened the envelope and found a letter of acceptance. "Sam," my mom said as she folded the letter back up, "I'll make you a deal. If you'll give this school one semester— just one semester—and you hate it, you can transfer to a different school. Besides, you can still play AAU basketball while you're there."

Ah, the Amateur Athletic Union. Every basketball student in urban America wanted to play AAU ball. It was like playing high school sports without the restrictions. NBA scouts came to the AAU games.

Mom was savvy, I must say. "Deal," I said, meaning it. "*One* semester, right?" I would stay at DeKalb for four years.

• • •

An interesting detail of the DeKalb School of the Arts was that most of the student body was of the female persuasion. I should have picked up on that detail during auditions, but I didn't register it that day. It's possible the whole reason I got into the school was that they needed more boys to balance out the hundreds upon hundreds of girls. Out of the three hundred kids in the school, maybe fifty were guys. And of those guys, maybe twenty-five were straight. Simple math will tell you that for every heterosexual guy, there were ten beautiful girls walking around in leotards all day. DSA was a conservatory, which meant that our athletic requirements all revolved around dance—ballet, to be precise. Yep, I took ballet. It was a requirement.

For a shy kid, man did I come into my own at DSA. So many life lessons learned, including navigating the mysteries of the opposite sex. If a young woman paid me *any* attention, I was overcome with nerves and joy, which would prove to be both my greatest source of confidence and yet my greatest source of pain.

During my junior year at DeKalb, I was coming from a Black History program in which I had performed, when I saw a friend I often flirted with. We said hello to each other and then locked eyes.

I had come to learn what that meant.

The decision I made next would change my life forever. It was a decision directly inspired by so many hip-hop lyrics running in my head, words of Tupac and others inviting me to seize the moment for "love."

65

There, in the middle of the hallway, things escalated. Nervous that someone would catch us embracing inappropriately, I took her by the hand and led her into the dark piano room. We only had a few minutes before we were expected in class, so whatever was going to happen needed to happen fast.

Moments before the "happening" happened, a teacher entered the room, saw what was about to happen, and started screaming. In an instant, I realized that everything I had been doing in the dark for close to a decade by that time was about to be revealed. The two lives I had been living out were going to be thrust into the open.

It wasn't long before I was seated in the principal's office being suspended for thirty-one days. "Effective immediately," the principal said. It seemed extreme, but maybe it was just what I needed.

Several years later, I started a podcast and TV show by the same name as this book—*A Greater Story*—and in the context of hosting it, I get to chat with all sorts of thought leaders, celebrities, musicians, actors, speakers, and more. During a particular interview with Brad Lomenick, one of the main architects behind the Catalyst Conference, one of the largest leadership gatherings in the world for Christian leaders, we discussed the secret to succeeding in life and with God. Brad flowed out of the concept of stewardship and said, "If you *crush* it in the now, it will lead to the next."[2] "Next" meaning something like the next level of your career, the next opportunity, the next elevated season.

But there, in the principal's office, I wasn't exactly *crushing* life. No, life was crushing me.

66

One of my favorite Bible characters is the apostle Paul. You probably are familiar with Paul's moment of transformation, which occurred when he was on his way to murder Christians living in Damascus. Jesus himself interrupted Saul and set him on a totally different path.

> He [Saul, who would be renamed Paul] fell to the ground and heard a voice saying to him, "Saul! Saul! Why are you persecuting me?"
>
> "Who are you, lord?" Saul asked.
>
> And the voice replied, "I am Jesus, the one you are persecuting! Now get up and go into the city, and you will be told what you must do." (Acts 9:4–6)

The passage in Acts goes on to say that the men who were traveling with Saul "stood speechless" because, while they definitely heard a voice, there was no visible speaker in sight (v. 7). I'd have been speechless too.

When Saul got up from the ground, the text says he opened his eyes but was blind. In fact, he stayed blind all the way into Damascus and for three full days following this occurrence. Once he made his way to the place God directed him, a man named Ananias approached Saul and explained that God had told him to lay hands on him. He lay hands on Saul, and "instantly something like scales fell from Saul's eyes, and he regained his sight" (Acts 9:18).

As my parents sat across from me at the kitchen table in our family home in Decatur the very same afternoon my secrets had been revealed, I had one of those scales-falling-from-the-eyes experiences. I had been living a secret life that was hurting not only me but others as well. Sin had become such a normal part of my lifestyle that I barely noticed it for what it was. Besides, all the kids were doing it. That meant it was okay, right?

The Bible says that God chastises those he loves. I was being chastised that day, for sure. My dad looked squarely at me, and without even a hint of shame in his voice, he simply said, "Son, it's on you now."

The "it" he was referring to was my *life*. My choices and the consequences of those choices. Dad explained, "Your mom and I have taught you everything you need to know to make it in this world. You know right from wrong and wrong from right. If you make a choice that destroys your future or one that drastically changes it, it's on you. I'm handing your life back to you."

Wow, what a moment. I was dumbfounded. He wanted *me* to live my life?

I got up from the table and walked silently back to my room, thinking to myself, *What just happened?* I sank down onto my bed and heard God speak to me for the first time. He said, "Sam, you have to choose. You can't serve two masters. Either you choose the dreams I have for you, or you choose the desires you have for yourself. You can't have both, Sam. It's either one or the other. And you've already seen where the other takes you."

I gave my life to Jesus that night. Without a preacher.

Without a worship leader.

Without a musician.

Without any "mood music."

Just a teenager, the audible voice of God, and the sinner's prayer.

• • •

When I returned to school after my thirty-one-day suspension, I didn't go near another girl for the rest of the year. For the first time, I was sitting in the driver's seat of my life. I was owning my choices. I was owning my responsibilities.

--------- • **REFLECTION** • ---------

Have you ever given your life to Christ? If so, what happened? What was it like? What led you there? What gave you the courage to do it? What changed after that? You know what's funny and consistently true about every person's salvation moment with the Lord? They always remember it like it was yesterday. Now I'm sure there are many reasons why that is, but perhaps the greatest reason is this: it impacts their soul.

Right? I mean, how could you forget something that impacts your soul? It's like forgetting the very first moment you fell in love. You wouldn't do that. Something in you changed that day, something within the part of you that normally didn't change. What I love about what happens to us when we surrender to God is that it always leads to more soul-shaking encounters that impact us forever. So if you've given your life to Christ already, keep on giving to him every day. If you haven't, let me ask you this: Do you want to feel your soul shake?

4

THE ROAD TO RESTORATION

*Failure is simply the opportunity to begin
again, this time more intelligently.*

HENRY FORD

Until I got myself suspended from DSA, my future was looking pretty bright. My immediate and extended family were
proud of me, and it had begun to look like their predictions
of me might come true. All the signs were hinting at success. I had grown from playing one instrument, the sax, to
mastering six. I was producing close to five beats a week on
the Triton. Local and aspiring artists were beginning to invite me into elite spaces to collaborate on music that would
debut on a national level.

Even DSA—before my debacle, anyway—had taken a liking to me. The school boasted many stars, including Donald Glover (also known as Childish Gambino), R&B superstar Lloyd, and a whole slew of Broadway performers. So when they began casting me in musicals, giving me premiere solos in the theatrical troupe, and pitching for media opportunities with the *Atlanta Journal Constitution* and HBO, I knew I'd arrived.

One day, the global entrepreneur, record executive, writer, and film producer Russell Simmons came to our school. This guy was *it*. Chairman and CEO of Rush Communications. Cofounder of the hip-hop music label Def Jam Recordings. Creator of the clothing fashion line Phat Farm. Simmons's net worth was estimated at $340 million in 2011, and he was coming to see *us*.

Evidently, Mr. Simmons was in the hunt for the next generation of HBO's *Def Poetry Jam* superstars. Despite poetry not being my forte, I prepared and performed a hybrid involving spoken word, singing, and playing the piano, and I was offered a spot in the upcoming showcase.

DSA was proud.

During my freshman year at the school, my friend Evan had told me about a group called the Freddie Hendricks Youth Ensemble of Atlanta. Tons of kids from DeKalb were part of the ensemble. Evan was an artistic big brother to me, and he explained that Freddie was the man I needed to know. I had untapped potential that could be realized under Freddie's tutelage.

I had to meet this man and join his crew.

Freddie was renowned in our community for having launched dozens of young men and women into the stratosphere of stardom, helping to prepare them for Broadway, *Saturday Night Live*, a whole host of record labels, and more.

Freddie's bio lists him as a graduate of Lincoln Memorial University, founder and former artistic director of the Freddie Hendricks Youth Ensemble of Atlanta (YEA), and producer of over twenty critically acclaimed productions that tackle contemporary issues such as child abuse, teen pregnancy, HIV and AIDS, youth violence, and apartheid. His bio also includes his many impressive accolades—such as distinguished teacher of America in Washington, DC, presented to him by President Bill Clinton in 1996 and 1998; an Abby Award for Lifetime Achievement in the Arts in 2002; Alumnus of the Year at Lincoln Memorial University; and many more. His international productions are numerous. However, Freddie's bio does not include that he has a keen sensitivity to the emotions and energy of people, especially the vulnerable population. I truly believe this trait helps to make Freddie a dynamic artist and artist mentor.

From Freddie's friends during the development stages of the Youth Ensemble, I learned of Freddie's intensity when he had created the award-winning musical *Soweto, Soweto, Soweto: A Township Is Calling!* (It's about the children in South Africa living under the apartheid regime.) He immersed himself in the history of apartheid. Through his research, Freddie discovered the Sharpeville massacre of 1960. This began as a demonstration against the Pass Law enforced on the Africans. The South African police opened fire on the crowd, killing sixty-nine people, including many children.[1] Looking at that number on the page and attaching that number to children shot by adults was more than Freddie could bear. The discovery brought him to tears. Any time Freddie learned about the abuse, neglect, or other evil done to children, it motivated him to use art to educate and ignite people to take a stand. His passion and dedication to use art to heal shines through.

Freddie's ensemble was the largest youth theater company in the world, and even today, some thirty years after its inception in the heart of Atlanta, it's still going strong under another name. The motivation of the ensemble was always "love" by way of creativity and activism—speaking up and showing up for the voiceless. Freddie always told us that he'd started the group in response to a vision God gave him. A vision of kids outside of his window, crying out for help, crying out to be saved. He believed that God assigned him this responsibility—to save a generation of young artists (us) by teaching us how to use our powers at the highest level for the betterment of society. "What good is art if it doesn't change the world?" he would always say. "Use your art for good."

Freddie was serious about that last piece. Instead of forcing preproduced musicals on his ensembles and casts, he would bring a challenge, a *societal ill*, to the group. He would "throw it in the soup," as he'd say, and ask us to stir. "Let it simmer. Let it sit. Build on it from there."

And as a result, things would be produced. Monologues. Scenes. Songs. Poems. Choreography. Ultimately, a full-length musical—every word, every transition, every beat. Freddie would do his due diligence to shape and mold the script, but he did nothing without input from his protégés. Later, after the musical was complete, we kids would travel with the show around the country and sometimes even overseas to perform it, in many cases, to critical acclaim.

During my residency with the ensemble, the most memorable topic Freddie brought to us centered on the intersection of South African apartheid and the AIDS pandemic. Two shows emerged from that topic: *Soweto, Soweto, Soweto: A Township Is Calling!* (version two) and *Times*. Freddie had deep compassion for the marginalized in our world. He had endured a rough childhood and knew what it was like to be cast aside, to suffer. He knew what it was like to not be able to trust the people who were supposed to lead you. He knew what it was like to need hope.

The process of understanding and becoming what was needed to birth these two shows as a primarily adolescent ensemble was transformative. Freddie believed in "method acting," but with a twist. Many scholars began to canonize Freddie's philosophy as separate from method acting, rooting it in what they would call "black acting methods." What this meant for us was that we were invited not merely to explore the world and its issues, but also to experience its pain. To do a Freddie show, in other words, you had to *become* what you were writing about. He would often say that it is impossible to become if you don't understand. So at any given moment, our rehearsal hall could turn into a real-life simulation of South Africa during the height of its oppression. People would be screaming at you, spitting on you, throwing chairs at your head. During *Times*, Freddie took our entire cast and crew to the AID Atlanta wellness center to learn about this global problem . . . and to take an AIDS test. We were sexually active teens, so it was one thing to hear the statistics; it was quite another to wait for those test results. If Freddie's approach sounds extreme, it's because it *was*. But it worked. That man taught us to think deeper, to love better, and to empathize instead of judge. His presence in my life forever marked me.

. . .

The first time I met Freddie, the first iteration of *Soweto* was touring. My school was supposed to go see the show, but I'd overslept and missed the bus. Dad had driven me straight to Freddie's theater for the show, and by the closing scene, my jaw was in my lap. This cast was *legit*. I ran to one of my friends in the ensemble who had just gotten off stage and said, "I've got to meet Freddie. Now." My buddy laughed and said, "I'll be right back."

Moments later, out walked the legend himself. "How are you?" he asked, sticking out his hand. I skipped the small talk. "Can you mentor me?" I asked.

Freddie laughed and asked me my name. From there, he took me through a series of tests to see if I was serious.

Show up for rehearsal at this time.

Write me a monologue about this.

Crank out a song here.

This went on for a few months, but once he realized I wasn't playing around, he invited me into the family.

The mentoring then began in earnest. Freddie began drawing leadership potential out of me, telling me I was going to "make it" someday. His favorite thing to say to me was, "Sam, you're going to be a preacher! I just know it! A *preacher*—that's who you are."

I should mention that while he was declaring me a preacher, he was also telling me that I was one of the best directors he'd ever seen and that I should absolutely keep pursuing stage work.

Who knew what I would become? I didn't. But regardless of the direction my life would take, Freddie was committed to preparing me for the best possible life I could live.

Early in our mentorship, I told Freddie that I had heard what he'd been able to do for black and Hispanic kids who came from nothing, and that I wanted him to show me how to be great.

"All right," Freddie said. "Let's start here."

Freddie placed a plastic water bottle on a table in an empty classroom in the rehearsal hall, while everyone else was rehearsing, and said, "I want you to stare at that water bottle for a full twenty minutes." He told me that if I took my eyes off of the bottle—even for one second—I had to start over. So, there I was, staring.

I may not have known much at age fourteen, but I knew one thing: This man was crazy.

In a recent research study, participants were asked to sit silently in a room that was empty except for a small device that was used to deliver a mild (but still painful) shock. During the pre-experiment interview, each of the participants had told researchers that they would pay good money to *not* be shocked during the experiment, and yet as time wore on, many of them—two-thirds of the men and one-fourth of the women— were so bored that they opted to deliver the shocks themselves, some of them multiple times.[2] Like this study, what my mentor was asking me to do was difficult and counterintuitive.

I messed up a few times and had to start over, but in the end, I prevailed. Freddie returned and asked me how I believed I did. I said, "I think I did okay. I'll be better next time."

"Cool," he said. "Keep at it. You'll get there."

This went on for two months until finally, I exploded. "You said you would make me great," I yelled, "and all you did was make me stare at water! Where's the greatness in *that*?"

"First of all, calm down," Freddie said. "Second, I *did* teach you something. I taught you how to focus. What have I always told you that any great artist who wants to excel needs?" He looked at me and waited.

"Focus," I said.

"Sam, focus is the ability to set your mind and heart on something and never turn away, no matter what obstacles may arise. That is what you just did. You *focused*. Don't you wanna be great, son?"

My mind was getting it. "Yes, sir."

"Good," he said. "Now let's get something to eat."

* * *

Years later, the apostle Paul's words in Philippians 3 would come to be deeply meaningful to me, for that's where he talks about *pressing on* to "possess that perfection for which Christ Jesus first possessed me. . . . Forgetting the past and looking forward to what lies ahead," Paul wrote, "I *press on* to reach the end of the race and receive the heavenly prize for which God, through Christ Jesus, is calling us" (vv. 12–14, emphasis mine). Freddie was teaching me to press on. Initially it was difficult to see, as are most lessons God teaches us on the way to the promise. I would later discover why this lesson was so important to catch.

By the time I got suspended during my junior year at DSA, I'd been sitting under Freddie's mentorship for two full years, no longer questioning his methods or ways. My current mentor and friend Reggie Joiner likes to remind those of us who help put on his annual student-ministry conference, Orange, that every child is just one caring adult away from thriving. And despite the oceans of acceptance, love, and support my parents did and still do pour over my life, Freddie was always that person for me.

On that fateful day at DSA, between being caught by the teacher and showing up in the principal's office, I escaped through the school's back door. I was terrified to face the consequences of my actions, just sure that life as I knew it was over. But something prompted me to go back inside; I knew deep down it was the right thing to do. I began making my way toward the principal's office but stopped about halfway, still questioning whether I should face my fate. The boys restroom became my hideout.

I pulled out my phone and called the only person I believed could help me. Freddie Hendricks picked up. "You *what*?" Freddie hollered, in response to my report, including a few choice words I'll leave out here.

"It's going to be okay," Freddie said. "The best thing to do is to face the music. You'll make it through this."

I had no idea how Freddie was so sure of this, but I desperately hoped he was right. I hung up and walked straight to the principal's office. And I took my punishment like a man. Freddie came and picked me up that day to drive me home.

The following morning, Freddie told me his plan. He was helping another school get a musical off the ground, and he could really use my help. He knew I had nowhere to be for the next month—so he said I should come with him.

The month I spent with Freddie and the students was week upon week of cleansing. The shame most would feel in that moment was replaced with tough love and acceptance. They were the shock absorbers for my grief, the laborers who selflessly rebuilt me when I'd been broken into pieces.

• • •

Heading into my senior year at DSA, the atmosphere was charged with anticipation. The faculty and students all knew about my massive mistake and that I had experienced a spiritual awakening of sorts. And while most were forgiving of my indiscretion, there were still some, such as the principal, who were very cautious regarding my return. That was certainly fair. I'd embarrassed myself. I'd embarrassed my family. I'd embarrassed the young woman I'd led astray. I thought I could finish at DSA, but the circumstances were just too tense so I left the school voluntarily. It was the right decision, and I needed to accept it. In the words of my cousins, "Sometimes, it be like that."

Two events had transpired over the summer that made this decision a little easier to swallow. First, I'd received a work-study job at Southwest Dekalb High School, where Sara was already going. I wouldn't have been able to take that job had I returned to DSA. And second, I'd landed my first record deal. I wasn't *quite* "Christian Usher," but hey, it was a deal.

The trend I was noticing was that whenever God wanted to grow me up in an area, he introduced a new champion into my life. In this case, it was Bishop Eddie L. Long of New Birth Missionary Baptist in Lithonia, Georgia.

Life was *good* for Bishop Long. He sat on or presided over the boards of directors for Morehouse School of Religion, North Carolina Central University, Young Life, Safehouse Outreach Ministries, and 100 Black Men of America. He served as the personal pastor to celebrities such as Usher, Ludacris, Tyler Perry, and Deion Sanders. And through various business ventures outside of the ministry, he was a very, very wealthy entrepreneur and investor.

I met Bishop Long two months after I gave my life to Jesus. As you may recall, my parents had released me into the wild of life and had given me sole ownership for my decisions. It had clicked in my mind that no one could make me be great but me, which is when I decided that if I was going to make me great, I'd better have some help. That's when I decided to turn things over to God.

The great thing about having someone like Freddie Hendricks constantly pouring into you as a teenager was that, while you may not always *apply* the wisdom, at least you *had* it. During the months between being handed my life back and meeting Bishop Long, what I heard in my brain was Freddie's voice: "Focus!" "Use your art for good!" "Don't wait to be great. Move now!"

So move I did. After giving my life to Christ, I exited my bedroom a true child of God and immediately started working on a demo to send to record labels. I called producers. I summoned friends to give feedback and called on collaborators to help me execute my vision for the project. One of those friends was a member of Bishop Long's mentorship program for young men, LongFellows Youth Academy.

At the time, Bishop was a celebrity, which meant that participation in his program was highly coveted. My buddy and I wrote a gospel song with an R&B feel, and once we cut it, I jokingly said to him, "We should let Bishop Long hear this!"

One week later, we were in Bishop's office, singing our new song for him and his executive staff.

From there, things escalated quickly. Bishop Long invited my friend and me to fly to New Orleans to perform our song for the 100 Black Men conference taking place there. Within two hours our flights were booked, and we were telling our parents about all the possibilities that lay ahead. Two days later, we were sitting in a pizza parlor with several of Bishop's team members when he said, "I will get you a record deal."

Across the next three months, I met gospel superstar Kirk Franklin and multiple Grammy Award–winning producer Rodney Jerkins. It felt like I was on a rocket ship. DSA was in my rearview mirror, and worldwide ministry lay ahead.

• • •

The New Birth season with Bishop Long lasted into my early twenties. Within that seven-year stint, I met presidents of countries, saw private planes come and go, and witnessed supernatural ministry taking place.

Thousands of lives were changed, and I knew I was part of something real. In fact, everything I know today about how to run a business, how to craft a strategic plan, how to get an idea off the ground, and how to collaborate with people, I learned at New Birth. I never wanted it to end. But end, it did.

In 2010 four of my friends from LongFellows filed a public lawsuit against our spiritual father, Bishop Eddie Long, claiming he had done some things to them that *no one* should have done to them. Suffice it to say, the entire ministry was shaken. Our city was shaken. Our faith was shaken too.

In less than twelve months' time, church attendance sank from 30,000 to 3,000, leaving New Birth feeling like a ghost town. I felt torn. Could Bishop Long actually do something as horrendous as what these claims said?

I found myself caught in between my brothers and my spiritual father. Attempting to honor everyone while remaining neutral wasn't the easiest of tasks. I will never forget that feeling.

Those were difficult days.

I stayed on at New Birth for just over a year, but eventually it was clear that the ministry was headed in a direction I could no longer lead in. Deciding that I wasn't the right guy to help lead them to that new place, I resigned. God would sort out this tangled mess . . . for me, for Bishop Long, for the church.

• REFLECTION •

Who do you become when life throws you a curveball? When the pressure is on, many of us tend to retreat. A lot of us combust; hence the need for counselors. When you're in a pressure-filled moment, or what I call "a turn," I've found that the best thing to do is to keep turning. Eventually, you'll come around the corner and things will get lighter. This is similar to the phrase, "When you're going through a storm, keep going. Eventually, you'll get to the other side." There is a light at the end of the tunnel, my friend. Trust me, I know.

5

WHEN FAITH IS TESTED

Often when I pray, I wonder if I am not posting letters to a non-existent address.

C. S. LEWIS

At twenty-three years old, I was longing for purpose and searching for a new path. Maybe it was time to return to my first love, R&B. Christian Usher—that had been the dream. For the previous seven years I'd surrendered my path to work at New Birth, serving as a licensed preacher, praise-team leader, and part-time youth pastor. But with that whole situation in ruins, I was eager to start afresh.

It was at New Birth that I'd learned about the importance of a musician's manager. Scores of famous musical acts had come through to perform, giving me a chance to see firsthand how vital a manager's role could be. I called an entertainment lawyer I had met and asked him to send me someone "epic." To my surprise, he did.

Jareiq was a young, ambitious Brit who was determined to get me to the top of the music industry . . . and fast. On the heels of an intense season that found us working in the studio until five in the morning most nights, writing and recording more than eighty new songs, we created dozens of electronic press kits and sent them out. We built libraries upon libraries of pictures of me. We consulted with influencers and industry experts. We booked every venue that would have me. We hustled. We hustled *hard*.

We'd put in the work, and yet still I was shocked when meetings with labels started to materialize.

Our first meeting was with Universal Canada, where Universal Worldwide Music Group is based. Twenty executives had asked three artists to come perform, in hopes of signing all of us in a joint venture. My performance felt like an out-of-body experience. I was in the *zone*. "They want you!" my manager shouted.

The problem, I would find out later, was that they didn't want the other two artists, and so within three months, the deal was dead.

Our second meeting was with the president of Motown—at the time, Sylvia Rhone, long regarded as the most influential female executive in the history of the music business. Due to some scheduling challenges that I think were explained when Sylvia showed up with her leg in a cast, our meeting had been delayed by weeks. But by the time we got there, I was ready to make history. I started singing one of my original songs, Usher inspired—just my manager, my guitar, and me—and I thought, *She's going to love this. This is the moment. . . .*

Sure enough, after I'd sung the last note and looked up at her, she was laughing and clapping her praise. "I loved it!" she said. "You're incredible! But I'm afraid I can't sign you."

She went on to explain that she had just signed someone who was "identical" to me—in voice, in range, in style. Sensing my unbelief, she pulled up a photo of the guy on her laptop, and just as she'd said, there I was. Or my identical twin.

Same age.

Same haircut.

Same glasses.

According to her, same sound. *What?* This was insane.

The third meeting took us to the Big Apple—New York City. At the designated time, my manager and I made our way to the top of a giant glass-and-steel building that overlooked all of Manhattan. Our meeting was with executives from MBK, the company that managed Alicia Keys. This place screamed creativity. I was soaring up with the clouds.

The meeting went well, and as the executive who had overseen the session escorted my manager and me back to the elevators, he looked at me, shook my hand, and said, "Keep making music. Let me meet with some of the other members of my team, and I'll get back to you."

Yes. This was good news. Well, at least this wasn't bad news.

Three months later, my manager and I flew back to New York, this time to perform at a showcase. I *killed* it in front of the audience the team had assembled, but when it was all said and done, the head of the management company approached me and said, "You were awesome, but bro, I'm so sorry. We can't sign another male artist right now."

I was floored.

A few years went by, and I was just about ready to throw in the towel on my dream of being Christian Usher when my manager called and said, "Let's give it one more try. One more showcase. In Atlanta. Devyne Stephens Studio, where Babyface records and rehearses. The only one on the ticket is you. I'll bring the entire Atlanta music executive presence out—Atlantic, Disney, everyone."

I knew better than to get my hopes up, but how could I say no to that?

"Never give up," Freddie had taught me. I told Jareiq I was in.

I arrived at the studio early, determined to create another Universal Canada performance. Some of my guys were there to help me set up audio, and as we were searching for the mics and mic stands, we realized that there were none to be found.

I called Jareiq and said, with as much self-control as I could muster, "Heeey bro, umm, did you reserve mics when you rented the studio? Because if you did, THEY AREN'T HERE."

He rushed down to the studio, gave the manager of the studio a piece of his mind, and then said to me, "Babyface took all of the mics down the street for a rehearsal, and no one told me. They forgot we were coming."

Babyface!!!

"What are we supposed to do?" I said, with a little more force than I intended.

"Go get some rentals—it's the only thing we *can* do. The showcase starts in an hour."

Three hundred dollars later, I had mics and stands in place. Which was the good news. The bad news was that the rental mics were evidently incompatible with the studio's sound system, which meant that feedback and that unforgettable microphone squealing were inevitable. So the mics were literally screaming at us. While the mics were still ringing, I noticed I didn't have my sustain pedal for the mini Triton I now used, and also there were no monitors in the room. During our (awful, terrible, couldn't-be-worse-than-it-was) sound check, neither my band nor I could stay on beat because we couldn't hear ourselves play or sing.

Eight minutes before the showcase was to begin, I ran downstairs to use the restroom, which was when I saw my dancers driving away through the back window. "Guys!" I hollered as I chased after them down the street, looking like a fool. "The show starts in five minutes! Where are you *going*?"

They hollered from the car, "We have another showcase! Sorry, Sam! We must have mixed up the times!"

I guess they knew how bad this showcase was going to be. I sure did. Only a fool could have missed those signs.

I was filled with despair as I headed back to the studio. But I took the stage and held things together as best I could. I probably don't have to tell you that it was the worst showcase of my life. The fact that it occurred in front of some of the most important music-industry decision makers in the country felt like life mocking me. When the night was over and I found myself back on my mom's couch that night, broke as a joke, I said it: "I think music is over."

• • •

Four gigantic opportunities.

Four elusive and mysterious nos.

I couldn't sort out what part of my present life was worth living, given how everything had gone.

I had worked so hard, and yet nothing was working. *Nothing* was working for me. I had given the church everything I had, and it had folded on me. I had given faith everything I had, and it had led me here. Freddie had told me to follow my passion. Bishop had told me to live right. Mom and Dad had told me to take control. Yet in the end all I had to show for those years was frustration and spiritual doubt.

Was God even real? Was he *here*?

Did he see me? Did he care?

As I sat on that couch, the rest of the world faded away. I needed answers, and I needed them now. I needed help like never before. I needed God front and center so that we could *talk* about some things.

"I've surrendered everything to you," I said to the room around me. "I've tried to grow the gifts you've given me. I've worked my tail off, chasing the opportunities you've put in my path. And nothing—*nothing!*—has panned out. What do you want me to do? Where do you want me to go? Why are you making me suffer like this?

"I'm broke.

"I'm still living with my parents.

"I'm desperate.

"I'm completely lost.

"Theologically, none of this makes sense to me anymore.

"None of this works.

"Is this what you wanted for me?"

I was mad at God. I was mad at the church. I was mad at this thing called life.

Somewhere in the recesses of my mind, I was taken back to a scene in the Bible where Jesus's disciples were lower than low. Those disciples had witnessed Jesus perform back-to-back miracles that fulfilled prophecies from long before, and yet now, when they needed him most, they felt abandoned by their powerful Lord.

Matthew says this:

Now when Jesus saw a crowd around Him, He gave orders to depart to the other side *of the sea.* Then a scribe came and said to Him, "Teacher, I will follow You wherever You go." Jesus said to him, "The foxes have holes and the birds of the air *have* nests, but the Son of Man has nowhere to lay His head." Another of the disciples said to Him, "Lord, permit me first to go and bury my father." But Jesus said to him, "Follow Me, and allow the dead to bury their own dead."

When He got into the boat, His disciples followed Him. And behold, there arose a great storm on the sea, so that the boat was being covered with the waves; but Jesus Himself was asleep. And they came to *Him* and woke Him, saying, "Save *us,* Lord; we are perishing!" He said to them, "Why are you afraid, you men of little faith?" Then He got up and rebuked the winds and the sea, and it became perfectly calm. The men were amazed, and said, "What kind of a man is this, that even the winds and the sea obey Him?" (8:18–27 NASB)

That last sentence stuck with me as I sat there on Mom and Dad's couch: *What kind of man is this, that even the winds and the sea obey Him?*

The disciples had blindly followed Jesus into a storm, and now, as the winds howled and the waves crashed around them, Jesus had the nerve to *sleep*. That was me. Smack dab in the middle of a storm, just sure that my Savior was nodding off.

The disciples immediately became frightened. "Lord, save us!" they cried. They were beckoning to the One who controlled the *universe*, and yet they were afraid of a little storm?

With a word, Jesus calmly reminded them that all was well. His silence didn't equal his absence.

He was still in complete control.

I learned that day that it truly was *control* that God was after in me. I truly believe that God will bring us to our lowest to strip us of our agenda. He is working at his fullest in us when we are surrendered. He was stripping me. He was at work.

"God, I feel like I'm losing!" I said to him while I was drowning in confusion. "I need you to make sense of this now! Bring me to heaven to be with you, because life here on earth feels like death." It was as if I was in the boat screaming at Jesus, "Save me!"

And God was saying, "Oh, ye of little faith."

In a voice barely above a whisper, God then spoke a statement that saved my life and rocked my world. One of Christianity's greatest young voices of today, Judah Smith, would call it a "rhema word"—a word that is rooted in Scripture but is delivered to you personally, for your specific situation.[1]

God said, "Son, if you can lose, then you can also win."

———• REFLECTION •———

What is God after in you? Is God stripping you of your agenda? Maybe for some of you it's already stripped away. For others, you and God may be in a wrestling match or around the corner from one. Let me save you some energy and time—just let him win. The quicker you let him win and release control, the easier life will be. Now that's easier said than done, but the premise still remains true.

PART TWO

· · ·

BY GOD'S AMAZING GRACE

6

KILLING IT,
BEFORE IT
KILLED ME

So let us come boldly to the throne of our gracious God.
There we will receive his mercy, and we will
find grace to help us when we need it most.

HEBREWS 4:16 (EMPHASIS MINE)

I discovered porn in the third grade. Or, I should say, it discovered me.

Sin always finds us. And if it doesn't find us, it creates more entry points than any other activity that has ever existed, which *feels* like it's looking for us. It's just so easy to sin.

It's easy to get drugs if you want them. It's easy to get a stripper if you want one.

And sadly, it's easy to find porn if you want to. In my case, it was easy even if you *didn't* want to. Looking back, it seems like porn was waiting on me, which is an idea that lines right up with what the Bible teaches. In the Scriptures, we learn that (a) we have a sin nature, (b) there is an enemy who loves to leverage sin in our lives, and (c) that enemy's ultimate goal is to utterly take us down—to destroy us, to kill us, to totally wipe us out.

When I was just a kid, before I started that hundred-shots-a-night ritual, I sought out a homie to invite into the mix, a friend to hang out with, someone to challenge in one-on-one. We may have only been third graders, but our battles were *intense*. Out there on the driveway, we'd be sweating and fouling and trash-talking each other like it was game seven of the NBA finals with three seconds left on the clock.

One afternoon, after four or five games, my friend and I were wiped. We needed a break. We needed some water. We headed toward his house.

Once we arrived, my friend's fifth-grade sister invited me upstairs to see what she was working on. I said, "Cool," and followed her up. What she was working on, I'd learn, was me. We had no sooner set foot in her bedroom when she spun on her heels, shut the door, and led me to her bed. "Look at this!" she said, as she unpaused a DVD. "Bet you've never seen *that*."

I couldn't have known what those images were unlocking in me—and at the tender age of eight. I must admit, while this kind of thing was *new* to me, it wasn't entirely unknown. I was reared on Tupac, Biggie Smalls, 112, Montell Jordan, Usher, Tyrese, Ginuwine, Jagged Edge, Siquó, Immature,

B2K, Too Short, Uncle Luke, Ludacris . . . the list goes on. Hip-hop. R&B. Rap. All the things. What's more, I would come to understand later in life that for at least *six generations*, lust has run rampant in my biological family. That stuff that our grandparents struggled with, it's a trigger for you and me.

I didn't know it until I faced it, but lust was a trigger for me.

From the third grade until high school, the lust I abided in my mind and heart just grew and grew and grew. So many women I took advantage of. So many women I'd have to eventually call and say, "I screwed up. Would you please forgive me? You are better than how I treated you."

Hip-hop could entertain me, I'd learn, but it couldn't teach me how to treat a woman. Only Jesus possessed those lessons. Only Jesus could show me how.

Making good on so many of his promises in Scripture, God would take a wounded, broken teenager in search of greatness and acceptance and radically strip him of his desires, his dreams, and the sting of his proclivities, to align him with his prewritten destiny. To introduce that young man to the greater story God had for him—the story that was his, alone, to live.

• • •

A friend once told me that the way to tell if you're in need of divine rescue is that you look at a certain habit in your life and realize that if you don't kill it, it will kill you.

These days, the more people I meet, the more strongly I believe that we all have a habit that needs to be killed. What

I've come to understand is that we *all* have a sinful tendency that if left unchecked will take us down.

Which begs the question, what do you struggle with?

Comparison?

Addiction?

Fear?

Doubt?

Maybe pride?

I may not know what your specific struggle is, but I do know one thing for sure: that struggle can be broken off of your life by the healing, saving power of God. As my friend and mentor Pastor Jeff Henderson likes to say, "When your story connects with God's story, it leads to a greater story."

Jeff is one of the lead pastors at North Point Ministries, under the leadership of Andy Stanley, and he is one of the main reasons that my ministry, A Greater Story, exists. That line of Jeff's—"when your story connects with God's story, it leads to a greater story"—became my mantra. It became my approach to everything. It became my TV show and podcast title, my book title, my *life*. "Connect to God's story!" I began infusing that message into youth groups and schools and church congregations and more. (More on that a little later.) "It's only by connecting to God's story that your story will come alive," I've told anyone who will listen. "It's only then that your story will *become*."

For the past decade, I've made my living telling people that despite what they believed their story was about—abandonment, addiction, graduating from high school, getting a promotion, finding true love, being adopted, reconciling with a loved one, or getting fit at the gym—I believe it's

all a part of God's plan. And that by deciding to co
with him intentionally, meaningfully, and enthusiastically,
they will find true purpose. "God is redeeming a broken
world," I've told people every chance I've had. "When we
forfeit our plans and join him in his magnificent work, we
experience *fulfillment*, for the

first
time
in
our
lives."

• • •

But how does this occur?

How did God make me into "Baby Jesus," as the students
began to call me back when I was completing high school at
Southwest Dekalb High School after leaving DSA? DSA had
called my month away "a suspension." Freddie had called
it "an opportunity" to help him. I called it "God saving me
before I destroyed myself."

I met Bishop Long. I got that first record deal . . . onward
and upward, I'd thought. But I was young. I was dumb. I
was gullible. Which is how I landed in the middle of a whole
slew of lawsuits with some record labels. If it wasn't for one
sincere music executive taking pity on me and agreeing to
mentor me, I would've lost myself.

After transitioning out of my dealings with Bishop Long
and leaving New Birth Church, in short order I found myself
in a tussling match with two millionaires/aspiring record

executives/dentists who had a lot of ambition but only a little knowledge of the business. They threatened they would not replace the fake tooth that had fallen out of my smile at IHOP if I didn't start doing songs again, even though I was broke because they'd stopped paying me the money they promised to give me so that I could eat.

In the middle of this mess, Freddie called. "Son," he said, "what are you doing?"

"I'm just sitting here," I said. "I'm broke. I'm stuck in a record deal. I'm in a lawsuit. And I'm toothless."

He said, "Bad day! Listen, come to California with me. I need you to help me direct another musical. Get away for a bit, while all that stuff works itself out. I'll *hire* you. You need some money, right?"

This was an easy yes.

While in Pasadena with Freddie, I sank into a deeply depressed state. I left the house we were staying in and felt a feeling I would never forget. Maybe you've felt this before. For the first time in my life, the thing that had brought me the closest to God now made me feel alone. The vision, the dream, the passion, the gift that I felt God placed in me and had been developing since I was six, he was no longer in. For the first time in over two decades of life, I didn't "feel God" in music anymore. I was walking along the sidewalk on a bright, sunny day when the realization swept over me, and I stopped and wept.

The shortest verse in the Bible is, "Jesus wept" (John 11:35 NKJV). And yet I think it's one of the strongest. Jesus's friends Mary and Martha had just lost their brother, Lazarus, and Jesus was nowhere to be found. They'd sent a messenger to ask Jesus to save their brother before it was too late, but Jesus had chosen not to come. Two days he waited, before he showed up. Two days!

Mary and Martha were distraught.

When Jesus did show up, the text says that he wept. He couldn't have been crying over Lazarus's death, because he could have *prevented* that death. No, he was crying because his friends were crying.

Their tears had moved him to tears. His delay in coming to his friends' aid was strategic; he would raise Lazarus from the dead, thus proving his supernatural power and gathering glory for God. But in the meantime, before that resurrection, his heart of compassion led him to weep.

The message for me and also for you? God will always care for us, even when what is hurting us is *his plan*.

What hurt the most for me that day on the sidewalk was not the realization that I didn't feel God in music anymore, but rather the fact that I knew that it was his plan to pull away. I knew it was right. I knew he was saying, "Son, it's time for something else."

Still, that moment was hard. This was my *lifelong dream* being stripped away. I had poured a million hours into writing songs and studying music. I had talked the talk. I had walked the walk. I had put in the work. I had put in the time.

Even now, as I type these words, tears spring to my eyes. God knew it was hard. God cared that it was hard. God cared for me in my pain. He held me the entire time, and he'll do the same for you.

Maybe you're stuck in a Lazarus moment right now, waiting on something to be raised up. Something is dying in your hands, and you're worried that death will have the final word. If that's you, please be encouraged. Trust God's plan while holding his hand.

I now know that God was stripping me that day. Music, while an amazing gift I'd been given, had become an idol. Sam the Recording Artist had become my identity. God was killing me so that he could live. He was ripping out the desire in me to make his plan fit into mine.

"I know you say you love me, Sam, but if I don't do it the way you want me to, will your love and devotion end?" This is what God was asking me. Or, in other words, "Am I in charge, or what?"

There in Pasadena, I threw up my hands and said, "I'll do whatever you want me to do, Lord. *Whatever* you want me to do. I don't ever have to do music again. I don't ever have to create another song. If you want me to work at McDonald's, become a schoolteacher, work as an auto mechanic, I'll do it! As long as you're with me in it."

Then, in a fit of commitment, I said, "Listen, Lord, whatever job offer I get next, I'm going to assume is from you and will pursue that direction with everything I've got!"

Ten seconds later, my phone rang.

"Hello?" I said, half-expecting it to be God himself on the line. "Sam, where are you at?"

It wasn't a job offer. It was my manager, ready to head to the airport and fly home. But *three weeks later*, my phone rang again, and this time, I was offered a job.

"You want me to do what?" I asked the pastor on the other end of the line.

"Be our choir director, Sam!" he said. "The choir director for our youth!"

The pastor was from Ebenezer Baptist Church, famous for having been the church where both Martin Luther King Jr. and his father, Martin Luther King Sr., served. I knew the church well; what Atlanta native didn't? Still: choir director? For their *youth*?

Maybe I should have been happy that God sent a job my way that had anything to do with music.

Instead, I fumed. I *hated* gospel music. I had progressed way *beyond* working with youth.

I thought back to the seemingly random occasion when I'd met this pastor. Just after returning home from California, Freddie had asked me to help him by doing a reading as part of one of his shows. Because (a) it was a paid gig, and (b) I was desperately in need of cash, I said yes. After the show, Freddie introduced me to some of the staff from Ebenezer who had come to see the performance, and this particular pastor said, "You've got a great voice!"

Now he wondered if I'd use that voice to help their kids learn how to sing.

"I'm an R&B artist!" I hollered to the air around me, after I'd graciously ended the call. Plus, what did I know about directing a choir, let alone a choir made up of *kids*?

You were part of a youth ensemble that sang for years, my conscience said to myself.

Whatever. That was then, and this was now.

An artist named Zach Williams released a song last year titled "Rescue Story," and part of the lyrics read, "You were the voice in the desert, calling me out in the dead of night." Later it talks about God being our rescue story. In that moment, when all I had was this *one opportunity* before me, this one chance to take a step forward in life, I felt exactly like those lyrics say . . . like I'd been in a dry desert wasteland, desperate for some sort of help.

Was this God calling to me, inviting me from darkness into the light? Was this really what my "rescue story" was going to look like? This was my immediate destiny? Seriously? *A gospel youth choir?*

I reached for my phone to call Ebenezer back, muttering, "God, this had better be good."

• REFLECTION •

Take a few moments to reflect on this question, "If God asked you to trade your dream for his, would you do it?" Maybe some of you have already done that, but maybe God is asking some of you to do so right now.

7

MY EBENEZER

If I only had a little humility, I would be perfect.

TED TURNER

God wages war on prideful people. At a minimum, he deals with them very, very aggressively. Throughout Scripture, we see God shut down leaders and followers of his who are filled with pride. If I had to pinpoint God's pet peeve, this is it. I've watched individuals who were pretty *jacked up* by our world's standards receive grace from God, while those who seemingly have it all together but are prideful suffer in inhumane ways. Am I the only one who has judged people who don't deserve what God has given them? You know what those people generally are? *Humble.* "God opposes the proud," James 4:6 says, "but gives grace to the humble."

If that verse doesn't rock you, nothing will. But have you ever stopped to ask why? What's so offensive about being prideful? Yes, it's bad, but *why*?

A short list comes to mind: Pride is the sin of Satan—the sin that got him kicked out of heaven, in fact. Pride is the root of *all other sin*, making it a gateway sin of sorts. Pride is what blocks God from penetrating our hearts to guide us, correct us, and love us.

Pride is a wretched, wretched thing, which is why God. Hates. Pride.

This understanding clicked into place for me the moment I set foot into Ebenezer to assume my new role. Oh, how often our God-given purpose is hiding right behind an invitation into obscurity. God uses humbling experiences to commence the shaping and pruning he must do to properly position us for our specific assignment.

• • •

My first day at Ebenezer, I arrived early. I set down the lyric sheets I'd brought and started to rearrange the chairs. I rolled the piano off to the side, so I could see the alto section, and then I waited.

Ten minutes later, a mom and her daughter walked into the choir room. The daughter was eleven years old and an alto, the mom explained, and very excited to learn how to sing. "I'll just sit off to the side during rehearsals, if you don't mind," the mom said.

"Sure!" I said, as I escorted her to a chair.

I then walked the girl over to her section and said, with a little too much eagerness, "Thank you *so much* for coming. The other kids will be here soon . . . don't worry!"

We waited.

And waited.

And waited.

No one else came.

I was weighing my options on what to do next, when I sensed a prompting from God. "Teach this little girl like there are thirty other kids here," he said. "Treat her with the utmost respect and honor. Give her your all."

I glanced at the mom—Angela, she'd said her name was—and then motioned with "choir hands" for the young lady to rise. For days, I'd been practicing that dramatic swoop upward of the director's hands, which tells the choir it's time to rise, and I wasn't about to let that work go to waste.

Farris rose, her sheet music in hand, and when I played her starting note on the piano, she actually hit it with her voice.

I warmed up the girl's voice, taught her a bit of the song I'd brought, and then, figuring we had plenty of time to kill, invited her to sit down with me for a minute. "Do you know what worship is?" I asked her. "Do you know *why* we worship God?"

When our time was up, I walked her over to Angela and wished them both a good evening. The mom looked at me and asked, "What's your name again? You did a good job here tonight."

I reintroduced myself, and then she said, "*Sam*. Well, thank you, Sam. We'll see you next week then." For weeks, the only person who showed up to my choir practices was Farris. And while her mom was always kind, she grew frustrated over the church's lack of interest in the youth choir. "This is ridiculous," Angela said one evening. "I'm going to encourage Pastor to make an announcement on Sunday to the entire congregation that the youth choir is back up and running, and *we need your kids*!"

The following week, thirty kids showed up. That night, the youth pastor stopped by. "What you got going on over here?" he said. "A lot of my kids are here, homie!"

He and I talked for a minute before I laughed and said, "Yeah, I was thinking it was just going to be me and Farris forever." I pointed across the room to the girl who had been my only choir member for four straight weeks, which is when the youth pastor said, "You know who that is, right?"

He studied my blank expression and said, "Her grandmother is Martin Luther King Jr.'s sister." I didn't try to hide my incredulity.

"Her mother is MLK's niece!"

I'd been giving private voice lessons to a member of Dr. King's family for four weeks and didn't know it.

Sometime after that revelation, the mom, Dr. Angela Watkins was her full name, pulled me aside during one of the ever-growing choir's rehearsals and said, "Sam, I don't want to negatively affect your work here with the choir, but I have a favor to ask you. My family will be taking some time to travel soon, and we wondered if you would come with us, so that our daughter could continue her training with you."

My primary role would simply be to give their daughter every advantage toward becoming the singer she longed to be. Aside from that task, I should consider myself their dear friend—like family—and join them for various outings whenever I wished.

Uh. Yes?

And so for two years, I traveled the country with MLK's niece and her family, training Farris in all things vocal performance, mentoring her in life, and having an absolute *ball*. Whenever possible, I politely and excitedly asked Dr. Watkins what it had been like to have Dr. King as an uncle, what her family's views were on ministry as a result of his influence, and what life was all about. Graciously, she indulged my every question, teaching me how to be an "adult" every step of the way.

Over time, our connection grew quite strong. "Sam," she said to me one day, "you need to be out there preaching what you've been teaching my daughter. Not the choir part— which is excellent, by the way—but the parts about worship, perseverance, faith. You can do this."

"You think so?" I said.

"Just think about it, Sam," Angela said. "*Dream*." Then she smiled and changed the subject.

• • •

During my stint with the Watkins family, I was still working with Ebenezer as the youth choir director, making what I would call a *modest* salary. Enough to put some gas in my car and eat but not enough to leave my parents' house. About a year into that arrangement, I decided to pay New Birth a visit to greet Bishop Long and thank him for helping me in my spiritual formation and for introducing me to the world of gospel music. Despite a bit of tension over my leaving the church, Bishop was happy to see me, and I was honored to see him.

"Sam!" he said when he saw me approaching him in the parking lot. "Man, how are you? It's good to see you doing well."

"I'm great, Bishop!" I said, taking in his new Maybach. "It's obvious *you're* doing well!" Say what you will about pastors driving fancy cars. Regardless, that Maybach was *dope*.

"What are you doing with your time these days, Sam?" he said.

"I'm a youth choir director," I said, trying to sound proud of my work.

"*A what?*" Bishop said as he eyed me with slight surprise.

I told him again, prompting him to say, "Why don't you come and do that for us?"

The offer from New Birth was equal to what I was making at Ebenezer, which meant I couldn't work at either place and afford to live on my own. In a burst of entrepreneurial insight, I asked both pastors if I could take both jobs, and thankfully, both said yes.

The arrangement served us all well, but only for a year. At that point, both pastors told me it was time for me to choose. The offer at each was to lead not only the youth choir but to oversee the youth arts ministries and production ministry as well. In the end, I chose New Birth.

• • •

While at New Birth, I met the daughter of Martin Luther King Jr., Dr. Bernice King. At the time, she had no idea I knew her cousin Angela. I would spot her walking the halls during the services and would randomly approach her, smile, and say, "I love you!"

She always laughed, blowing it off, but I meant what I said. Seeing her was like seeing the in-person embodiment of her parents. What a legacy they both left.

During my time at New Birth, Bernice's sister, Yolanda King, died. Bernice wanted to put together a song selection for the funeral, merging one of Yolanda's sermons into a prerecorded Israel Houghton song. It was nostalgic. She needed a studio and a studio engineer to bring it to life for her in this emotional time. She called Bishop Long's son, Edward Long, whom I knew well, and asked if he could help her out with the studio and some engineering. He agreed but explained that because of a prior commitment, he couldn't be at the funeral in person.

Then, he called me.

When I heard the knock on my door, I opened it to find standing there Dr. Bernice King and her best friend, De'Leice Drane.

For the next two hours, the three of us edited Yolanda's words, perfecting everything ahead of the eulogy later that day, which Bernice would do. What an honor it was to be a part of that time. I was changed, right there in that room.

When the night was over, I walked them to the elevator, we laughed with one another, and they said, "Don't be a stranger. God has his hand on you. Keep up the good work, Sam."

And with that, the elevator doors closed.

──• REFLECTION •──

For one reason or another, God has decided to take us low before going high. We find our way in the pasture, the alleyway, the back of the room. While many of us know this is true, we still tend to fight it. Our ambition or desire to be great often blinds us from the beauty of staying low. Humility is God's weapon of choice for sculpting his greatest vessels.

8

NO LOSING

If life is a game, you can win. You don't have to lose.

SAM COLLIER

What did God mean that night when he said, "If you can lose, then you can also win"?

Looking back on that day when I sat on my mother's couch drowning in sorrow, I remember doing some real wrestling with God. I thought a lot about winning. I thought a lot about losing. And slowly, I felt hope rise in my soul. What had been utter darkness was rimmed by a glimmer of light. I had been on the verge of suicide, and yet now I saw a way out. It's one thing to be depressed by life, but quite another thing to be depressed by the church. The church represents *God*, so to be disappointed by the church is to experience disappointment in God.

I asked God why he had given me so many dreams and no way to fulfill them, and in response, he showed me that I wasn't angry with anything the church had done but rather with something the church *hadn't* done.

I started to understand that it was what I didn't know that was killing me. I began to ask the question, "What didn't I know that I should have?" That question would lead me down a path that started to reveal the "mysteries of the kingdom," as Jesus called them—things that were right before my eyes that I did not see and that the church here in America hadn't shown me. It was like a scene from the Chronicles of Narnia: everywhere I turned, I found a new treasure. It was a series of extreme fact findings and connecting of dots. A study of human behavior with a contrast of scriptural consistency. I would find those who were "winning" with Jesus in a certain area and reverse engineer how they got there. I started to "work out my salvation," as the Scripture encourages us to do (see Phil. 2:12 NASB).

It was the best decision I'd ever made.

The verse that became the foundation for my radical shift in thinking is found in John 10:10, which says: "The thief does not come except to steal, and to kill, and to destroy. I [Jesus] have come that they may have life, and that they may have it more abundantly" (NKJV).

In the original Greek language, that word "abundant" means *advantage*. What Jesus was saying was that he had come so that we might live life with an advantage.

This was mind-blowing news to me.

"If you can lose," God had said to me, "then you can also win." Jesus had come to give me an advantage. Jesus had come to help me win. In the words of DJ Khalid, God had just dropped a major key on me. We're in a game with a real, live opponent. The enemy, the devil, forces of darkness. And yet, because of Jesus, we can *win*. Yes, the enemy seeks to kill and destroy, but Jesus longs to bring us life! He longs to bring us victory! He longs to bring us the *win*.

Because of Jesus, we can spread the Good News of the kingdom. Because of Jesus, we can tell people about grace.

Because of Jesus, we can spread love in the world. Because of Jesus, we can find our purpose in life.

Because of Jesus, we can take care of our family, we can take care of each other, we can defeat racism, we can defeat sexism, we can defeat poverty and sickness and low self-esteem. Because of Jesus, we can overcome gang activity, and violence, and child slavery, and greed. Yes, the enemy is playing against us, but in Jesus, *we have the win*. In Jesus, *we never lose*. I needed that word just then.

No Losing, Inc., was born out of a place of desperation. It was born for students, young adults, and adults who find themselves in a losing situation—which has been all of us at one point or another. What we discovered through the nonprofit was that losing was a state of mind more than it was a circumstance. And when your mind changed, your circumstances eventually followed.

My colleagues and I built school programs. We threw parties. We created what we called "success incubators." We dropped albums. We hosted breakfasts. We worked, and worked, and worked.

Five years into this work, we had reached more than one hundred thousand students in the inner cities and rural towns of Georgia, New York, Louisiana, and North Carolina with the mainstream message of No Losing.

We created the No C Campaign, which increased academic achievement by 50 percent in select middle schools around America. We successfully journeyed with seventy Christian young adults for five years and helped forty of them transition into their God-given calling. We did our best to serve Jesus well. And yet, despite all that work and all those successes, every good thing must come to an end.

I look back now and see that through every loss—my music ambitions, my church by way of scandal, my nonprofit— God was there to spur me on, always prompting me to keep his main thing my main thing, instead of letting *my* will, *my* way, take control.

I knew that I couldn't keep self-funding my nonprofit, but did that mean its message had to die? I knew the answer was no, and so I reached out to anyone and everyone I thought could help me revive its cause. I had learned that if God has ordained a direction or project, then he will provide for it, so we must position ourselves to receive that provision. I had also learned that said "positioning" takes *movement*, great *vision*, and *faith*.

God taught me that dreaming small within the confines of his will wasn't an option. His Word says he desires to do exceedingly and abundantly more than we can even ask or think. "Dream big!" he essentially tells us. "Dream big within my will."

I decided to reach out to Bernice King. It was a stretch, but not for God. I found her best friend's number, which

I'd been given during that studio session, and was shocked when she agreed to meet.

"If it's in your will, you bless it," I said to God after disconnecting the call.

When I pulled into Applebee's to meet De'Leice, I had a proposal in hand. She and I found our table and sat down to talk when all the power in the place went off. There was a terrific thunderstorm rolling through the area, and De'Leice and I took it as a sign. "God is up to *something*," she said with a grin. I couldn't help but agree.

On the heels of that meeting, Bernice and I met, and for the next three years, she and I teamed up on reaching the next generation. We worked with the King Center to launch assemblies that carried the No Losing message to more and more schools.

During the year that I transitioned No Losing to its new home, I steered clear of the church. I had learned how to be a man at church. I had learned how to run a business at church. I had learned how to have healthy relationships at church. Now that my church was gone, I felt sort of gone myself. I needed a change of pace.

A friend called one day and said, "Sam, if you want to see a ministry that is doing truly innovative things, you should go see what Andy Stanley's got going on at North Point."

I'd never heard of Andy Stanley, but I went. I fell in love with the church. I met a man named Chris Green there. And I never looked back.

Chris was the music director at North Point and also my first white friend. For the next two years, he and I went out to lunch together every two weeks and asked each other questions about race. We became best friends over those meals, growing in our own understanding, developing new paradigms.

I invited Chris to be on the revamped No Losing, Inc., board of directors, and right after he said yes, he said, "I should invite Andy down to meet you and hear about what you're doing."

Chris had been promoted to a senior leadership role over at North Point's second largest campus and had easy access to Andy.

"I'd love that," I said, meaning it. My respect for Andy was already off the charts.

With that meeting in mind, I invited Bernice King to join us. That meeting led to my joining North Point Ministries, a forty-thousand-member church, as a speaker, consultant, and host. That singular organization would launch me into greater ministry opportunities for six years (and counting), solidifying me as a voice of influence for the kingdom of God.

If life is a game, you can win. You don't have to lose.

By God's grace, the advantage is ours.

<hr>

• REFLECTION •

When you think about your life, do you see beyond where you are? Can you imagine a new reality in the midst of what would seem like a valley of despair? Do you allow brokenness and lack to define you, or do you allow it to motivate you?

This is the greatest battle we can ever fight. The fight for the future. The fight for a better tomorrow. Many believe that self-help books, exposure to opportunity, or simply access to education are the only ways to overcome circumstantial despair, much like the reality I found myself living, my rock bottom.

While it is not my goal to compete with or reject those ideologies, I must say that I disagree. I believe wholeheartedly that the only way to win in this life—no matter where you live in this world, no matter how dark your situation—is through the power of Jesus Christ. He is our only way out! Practically, intellectually, circumstantially, and of course spiritually. God gives us the advantage through Jesus. It is his Word that reveals to us the mysteries of this world that we live in—the cheat codes, if you will. He renews our minds, and as a result he creates possibilities where there were none.

A philosopher once said, "Many times it is not our situation that changes, it is us within our situations that change. And ultimately our situation changes as a result." Friends, when we change our mind, we change our life. We win. My encouragement to you today is to allow Jesus to illuminate your mind in such a way that you begin to see beyond your scarcity, hardships, and deficits and into a world of abundance.

9

A GOD DREAM

Every great dream begins with a dreamer.

HARRIET TUBMAN

I'm going to shoot straight with you. I love the church. I grew up in the church. I have basically served in one church or another since I was seven years old. I love the church! I love its vision. I love its mission. I love its faithfulness. I love its vibe. It's possible I don't love anything here on planet earth more than the church, the incredible bride of Christ.

And yet . . . there's also something I *don't love* about the church.

That thing I don't love? It's this: We as the church have failed in our efforts to teach people how to truly activate the new life they find in Christ. I love what a pastor friend of mine often says: "Salvation is only the door to the kingdom. Why would we just stop at the door and never actually go inside?"

Unfortunately, we as a church have failed to help people step inside the life God has for them to live and use their specific gifts.

This is a problem. A big one.

. . .

Let me draw our attention for a moment to God's words in the book of Jeremiah. Now admittedly, these words were spoken to a specific man—to Jeremiah. They weren't spoken to you and me. What I want to do by looking at these words is not focus so much on the specific application but rather on the general approach we can find.

Jeremiah was going about his business in his day and age, following the laws of the rulers of the day, when God interrupted his personal story with a message from on high:

> The LORD gave me this message:
>
>> "I knew you before I formed you in your mother's
>> womb.
>> Before you were born I set you apart
>> and appointed you as my prophet to the nations."
>> (Jer. 1: 4–5)

"I knew you."

"I set you apart."

"I . . . appointed you as my prophet to the nations."

Hang on to those thoughts for a moment. We'll come back to them. First, Jeremiah's response: "O Sovereign LORD," Jeremiah said, "I can't speak for you! I'm too young!" To which God replied, "Don't say, 'I'm too young,' for you must

124

go wherever I send you and say whatever I tell you. And don't be afraid of the people, for I will be with you and will protect you. I, the LORD, have spoken!" (vv. 6–8).

The text says that God then reached out, touched the prophet's lips, and literally put words in his mouth. "Today," God said, "I appoint you to stand up against nations and kingdoms. Some you must uproot and tear down, destroy and overthrow. Others you must build up and plant" (v. 10). God showed Jeremiah a series of visions so that he could *see himself executing* this plan of God's. Then, it was time to move. "Get up," God told him, "and prepare for action" (v. 17).

Let's go.

Let's *go*!

Observing the fearful young man, God then offered a final word of encouragement: "For see," he said, "today I have made you strong like a fortified city that cannot be captured, like an iron pillar or a bronze wall. You will stand against the whole land—the kings, officials, priests, and people of Judah. They will fight you, but they will fail. For I am with you, and I will take care of you. I, the LORD, have spoken!" (vv. 18–19).

God reminded Jeremiah who he was and still is, as well as what God had already done for him . . . I knew you, Jeremiah! I set you apart. I appointed you for a specific purpose in your generation, in your time. God put words in his mouth so that he could go change the world. God assured his beloved Jeremiah that he would take care of him until the end. Was this message directed specifically toward Jeremiah? It was. Are those three main tenets valid for you and me? One hundred percent.

. . .

During the No Losing years, I had an epiphany. Although I had heard various pastors teach that God had a purpose for me, I'd never been taught how to sort out what it *was*. By extension, I'd also never been taught how to sort out what it was not. This is why I felt like a failure, why I was *losing* during those years.

For the hundredth time, I came across that passage from Jeremiah. And between seeing God's message to Jeremiah with fresh eyes and hearing a preacher I deeply respect speak on the topic of life purpose, my vision began to clear. That preacher was Bishop Jakes, and here is what he said: "Most of us spend only 20 percent of our time doing what we're really good at and 80 percent doing what we think we're good at. And people *deal* with the 80 just to get the 20."

Twenty percent effectiveness. Eighty percent noneffectiveness.

Twenty percent God-breathed. Eighty percent self-imposed.

Twenty percent grace. Eighty percent hard work.

Jakes's questions were these: "What if we were to flip the figures? What if we could be effective, operating in our grace or God zone, 80 percent of the time instead of just 20?"[1]

Bishop Jakes went on to talk about the value of treating every moment as a gift, the importance of outsourcing things that other people can do, and so forth, but I couldn't shake his original premise: What if we *could* spend nearly all of our waking hours living "on purpose and in purpose" for God?

I was floored, wrecked, challenged, grateful. The question then became, "How do I discover my 20 percent?"

126

• • •

I'm going to spend the majority of this chapter walking through the definition of "purpose" that has begun to emerge for me over the past five years. It's a definition that I have continued to refine, based on dozens of coaching sessions with seekers, family members, friends—anyone in my life who has felt stuck in regard to their purpose.

What is purpose? What is *your* purpose? How do we pursue our purpose in life? Once we find it, how do we stay on course?

These are the questions I'm interested in answering together. Before we head there, let me give you my definition up front. Here goes: You discover purpose when PASSION, GIFTING, and PROVISION collide! In other words: *Your purpose equals your passion, plus your gifting, plus God's provision in your life.* If you're a visual person, then you'll like this version better.

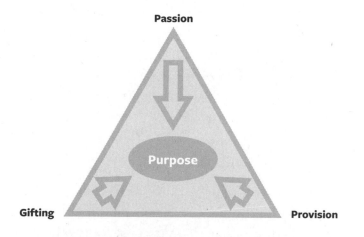

Now let's work through each part in turn.

Whose Purpose Do We Pursue?

You may have noticed in the passage from Jeremiah 1 that we looked at earlier that God frequently uses the pronoun "I."

"*I* knew you," he said to Jeremiah.

"*I* formed you."

"*I* set you apart."

"*I* . . . appointed you."

Likewise, throughout Scripture, we see God taking center stage:

- "'For I know the plans I have for you,' says the LORD. 'They are plans for good and not for disaster, to give you a future and a hope'" (Jer. 29:11).
- "Seek the Kingdom of God above all else, and live righteously, and he will give you everything you need" (Matt. 6:33).
- "You must not have any other god but me" (Exod. 20:3).
- "You are a chosen people. You are royal priests, a holy nation, God's very own possession" (1 Pet. 2:9).
- "You can make many plans, but the LORD's purpose will prevail" (Prov. 19:21).
- "But the LORD's plans stand firm forever; his intentions can never be shaken" (Ps. 33:11).
- "And we know that God causes everything to work together for the good of those who love God and are called according to his purpose for them" (Rom. 8:28).

128

We could keep going, but the point would be the same: *The believer's purpose belongs to God.* Just as was the case for Jeremiah, it is God who formed us. It is God who made us. It is God who called us, setting us apart. And it is God who purposes us. You and I were made *on purpose, for a purpose,* and that *purpose is found only in him.*

As a teenager, I didn't get this.

In fact, 99 percent of the people I've talked to—even those who grew up in the church—didn't get this. In most cases, they *still* don't get it, which is why so often they're found spinning their wheels. We good church folk think that passion should win the day. If we love *Jesus,* and if we're *passionate* about something, then poof! We've found our purpose in life.

The news flash is this: *It doesn't work that way.* There's more to the story than that, which brings me to the first element of the kind of purpose Scripture lays out: *passion.*

What Are You Passionate about . . . Really?

In asking people what they're passionate about, I've heard all sorts of replies. They'll tell me of the hobbies they're passionate about: singing, reading, cooking, hiking, weight-lifting, running, knitting, mastering the sax.

They tell me about loved ones they're passionate about: their spouse, their kids, their siblings, their friends, their work associates, their dog.

They tell me about business sectors they're passionate about: nursing, songwriting, teaching, writing, amateur sports, corporate leadership, their latest side hustle.

They tell me about personal goals they're passionate about: becoming (and then staying) debt free, reading the complete works of a particular author, training for and running a marathon.

They tell me about existential goals they're passionate about: becoming a more accepting person, learning to practice patience in stressful situations, being kinder to their kids, not being so stingy with money.

There are so many ways to take this question of what a person is passionate about, right?

I wonder, which direction would you take it? What are *you* passionate about? If we were sitting across from each other, and I said, "Tell me, what are you most passionate about?" I wonder what you'd say. Your family? Your friends? Volunteering in some capacity? Following a sports team? Something else?

Now suppose I asked you to take the top two or three things you're passionate about—the direct objects of your strongest passion—and craft a *life purpose* around those things. Could you do it? How would that life purpose read? Tough exercise, right?

Herein lies the problem: because the church has left a void regarding how to practically apply the promise that "God has a purpose for our lives," most people I know inside the church have been relegated to looking to the world to tell us how to do so. And guess what the world says to do?

"Follow your passion!"

"Be yourself!"

"You be you!"

"Live your best life!"

These mantras sound awesome, don't they? Yes! Follow my passion! Got it! Just be me! Never give up on me! Turn up! I'm here for that! Truly, who *doesn't* want to live their best life?

Perhaps you see the problem that's surfacing. On one hand, we have God saying, "I formed you, I made you, I gifted you, I knitted you together, I called you, I set you apart, I appointed you for good works, and I purposed you to accomplish things in my name."

Remember, our purpose as believers belongs to God. So that's one hand. But on the other hand, because we were never *really* taught how to find that purpose and fulfill that purpose, we started buying the lie that our purpose is somehow equal to whatever we feel passionate about. We started believing that the path to our purpose was paved with "following our heart."

Which would be fine except that's not at all how it works.

Rather than asking what we're passionate about and building our life purpose around that, we'd be better off asking which of God's passions fire us up most and building our purpose around *that*.

I was working with one of my closest friends within No Losing on finding and fulfilling her life's purpose, and to start, we were trying to sort out this "passion" thing. The question I landed on that I subsequently have used dozens of times is this: "If you learned that you had only one week to live, and God said that he would solve one problem through you, what problem would you pick?"

When I put it that way, her answer *flew* out of her lips: "I would empower young girls and women and eradicate the trafficking of little girls. *That's* what I'd do."

Now at the time, she was a hip-hop artist, an actress, an author, a professional speaker, and a radio personality. Guess what she was *not*? An activist. An educator. A legal advocate. The owner of a conference. The founder of a nonprofit that empowers and frees women and girls all around the world. On paper, it didn't look at all like this passion should belong to her. And in a manner of speaking, it didn't belong to her; it belonged to God and was being made manifest *through* her. Thus, none of the typical human-nature restraints and constrictions applied. If God wanted to use her to help free and empower women and girls, then God would do it, regardless of what anyone thought, said, or did.

I will tell you that after consulting with a group of beloved friends, family members, and colleagues, and after thoroughly praying through the decision, she *did* start a nonprofit. She *did* start a conference. She *did* become an activist. She *did* start to change the world!

Are You Great, or Are You *Graced*?

This step that my friend took, expanding her "purpose pursuit" to include people who love her, is a critical one. Ten out of ten times that I work with someone to help them find their life purpose, it is the *most* critical step they take. Here's why: without others' input, you can spend an entire lifetime thinking that the truest value that you bring to the world is something different than *what it is*. In other words, you could think that what you're doing is helping the world, while the only one being helped is you.

I like to think of it this way: There may be obvious things that you're great at. Along the way, I was told that I was "great" at singing, "great" at playing music, "great" at stage direction, and so forth. I probably *was* great at these things, from an earthly, temporal perspective. The question I didn't know to ask back then was, "Am I also *graced* at this particular thing?"

Nearly every person I talk with about these ideas tells me that upon closer reflection of their experiences thus far, they can look back and see times when the script of their life story was flipped. They were moving forward along a certain path, doing their thing, when something *totally unexpected happened*, something that completely upended their world. It was a "God moment"—that's what I've come to call them—those moments when the only explanation for what just took place was that Someone somewhere intervened.

For me, meeting Freddie was a God moment. Having Freddie tell me that first time that I was going to be a preacher someday—that was a God moment too. I remember thinking, *A preacher? What are you talking about? Can't you see I'm an R&B star?*

A Christian Usher—*that* was my destiny. I was a singer. I was a dancer. I was a *performer* at heart. I was in a *theater company*, not a seminary. I wrote songs, not sermons, for fun.

But then came that series of failed attempts with those music labels . . . and that trip to California . . . and the awful realization that God wasn't in my music anymore. The call from Ebenezer: a God moment. Meeting Dr. Watkins: a God moment. Then meeting Bernice King: a God moment, for *sure*. Being invited into so many urban schools: God moment, God moment, God moment. More God moments than my heart could hold. But even as it's easy to see those moments for what they are today, at the time, all I felt was grief. Still today, I work with people all over the world on these concepts, and the common dilemma they face is not knowing what to do with the fact that what they've *given their whole life to* is not God's purpose for them.

They were "great" at leading teams. They were "great" at teaching kids. They were "great" at doing deals. They were "great" at making art. They were "great" at any number of admirable things. It's just that they weren't also *graced*. In other words, while their *thing* may have been *all that* and more, that thing was doing nothing to accomplish the redemptive purposes of God. Remember: the purpose of our *true* gifting—those aspects of our work that aren't just *great* but also *graced*—is to build up the body of believers, and in so doing, to contribute to God's work in the world. Romans 12 says,

> Just as our bodies have many parts and each part has a special function, so it is with Christ's body. We are many parts of one body, and we all belong to each other.
>
> In his grace, God has given us different gifts for doing certain things well. So if God has given you the ability to prophesy, speak out with as much faith as God has given you. If your gift is serving others, serve them well. If you are a teacher, teach well. If your gift is to encourage others, be encouraging. If it is giving, give generously. If God has given you leadership ability, take the responsibility seriously. And if you have a gift for showing kindness to others, do it gladly. (vv. 4–8)

Ephesians 2 reminds us that it is *God* who initiates all forward momentum in our lives, not us. It is he who saves, envisions, fulfills. "God saved you by his grace when you believed. And you can't take credit for this; it is a gift from God. Salvation is not a reward for the good things we have done, so none of us can boast about it. For we are God's masterpiece. He has created us anew in Christ Jesus, so we can do the good things he planned for us long ago" (vv. 8–10).

Did you catch that last part? He made *plans* for us long ago. Plans for our welfare, we read in Jeremiah 29:11. Plans for *others'* welfare too. In fact, it's often this "others-centered" aspect of our gifting that reveals to us what is "graced." When I began asking people who love me and long for me to succeed what they believed my greatest gifts were, here is what I heard time and time again: "You're definitely incredible with music, Sam, but if I'm honest with you, the most powerful part of your performances is those moments *between your songs*, when you talk."

One friend said it with more directness still: "You're a great singer, bro, but that's not what's special about you. What's special about you is your ability to inspire through the spoken word, not through music."

Whew. That was hard for me. That was news to me. But God was speaking to me through that news. I could be great at singing—and maybe I was. But was my singing ability *graced by God* to fulfill his specific purposes for me?

The people I asked were real with me and revealed to me lovingly that the answer was no.

Find three or four trusted loved ones. One by one, ask them, "What is special about me?" Let them get all their emotionally charged, lovey-dovey remarks out regarding how kind you are, how loving you are, how amazing you are, how beautiful or handsome you are, and so forth. Smile. Say thank you. Give them a hug. Then, write all of that down and circle the similarities. This will be the heart of the gift God has *graced* you in.

You are a great . . . Listener. Inspirer. Activator. Shepherd. Processor. Planner. Friend.

Then, ask this: "What special gifts or talents do you believe are most valuable in me?" *Now* you'll hear some life-changing truth. My advice to you as these conversations unfold? Lean in. Listen well. Take good notes. Then, get alone with God for an hour and do the same as you did following the first question. Write it down. Circle the similarities. Sort out what's common in the input you've received. What are the bread crumbs God's asking you to follow? You'll find your grace gift in the words circled multiple times.

For me, it was *inspiration* and *speaking.*

For you it may be *shepherding* and *preaching. Planning* and *administration. Creativity* and *cooking. Determination* and *basketball. Encouragement* and *explaining medicine.*

Those clues will lead you to God's provision for you.

What God Graces, He Provides For

Recently I watched the 2004 movie *The Passion of the Christ,* which depicts the twelve hours of Jesus's life leading up to his brutal crucifixion in Jerusalem. I had seen it several times before but came back to it again to recenter myself on just how far Jesus was willing to go to connect you and me to God.

Back when I was a misbehaving kid, I'd say to my dad, "I love you, Dad. I love you *so much*," to which my dad would say, "Then act like it, Sam. Don't just *say* you love me. *Show* it."

Whenever I watch *The Passion of the Christ*, I think of that sentiment. Instead of just telling us how much he loves us, Jesus showed it. He showed it in a deeply significant way.

When Jesus endured whippings and beatings, he was showing his love for us. When he absorbed the mockery of his enemies, he was showing his love for us.

When he carried his own cross to the site of his crucifixion, he was showing his love for us.

When he was nailed to those wooden beams, flesh and bone ripped by each metal spike, he was showing his love for us. When he suffered for six full hours, eventually dying from the agony of it all, he was showing his love for us.

At each step in the process of Jesus humbling himself in obedience to God and dying a "criminal's death on a cross," as Philippians 2:8 says, God showed his great love for us. In this *ultimate act of provision*, God tended to our most basic need: our connection to him. Uninterrupted communion with our heavenly Father—that is the purest need we know. Now what does all of this have to do with your life purpose? With discovering who God made you to be?

The third component of our life purpose is God's provision—meaning, his sustaining power in our lives. If God has given you *passion* for something and has *graced* you in that thing, then he will *provide* for its success day by day. How do we know this is true? Because he already gave everything for us.

God saw us in our sinfulness and offered to rescue us. God was patient with us, not wanting any of us to have to live separated from him. God appeared in loving-kindness, dealing mercifully with us. God gave us the gift of eternal life, if only we'd believe. God gave us the hope of heaven, of eternity spent with him. God promised that he'd always be with us, making us more like him every day. "Whatever is good and perfect is a gift coming down to us from God our Father," James 1:17 says, "who created all the lights in the heavens. He never changes or casts a shifting shadow." Any good and worthwhile provision we enjoy, we enjoy because *God* put it there.

We see God in the Old Testament consistently providing whenever his people were in his will and were in need. We see him consistently providing for his followers through Jesus by the feeding of the five thousand. They were following him, they were living in his will, and he provided. Even the apostles who were launched into the world to accomplish the Great Commission always had what they needed to get the job done. *Always.* Which means that wherever we're *not* experiencing provision, we have no business being there.

Once I sorted out that God's purpose for me centered not on music but on preaching, teaching, and speaking, I went full force in that direction. I accepted every speaking engagement I could find. I locked in with North Point Ministries. I stayed up through the night practicing, reciting, studying

Scripture, searching my heart, and doing my best to master the presentation of these sermons and talks.

Later, I invested in videographers who had expensive cameras and lights. I paid editors to help me put together reels of me teaching, interviewing interesting people, and coaching people toward their purpose in life. As God provided further opportunity, I stepped into it. And I'll keep going until God tells me to stop. Interestingly, he still hasn't uttered that word. He continues to provide on this path.

· · ·

Recently, I interviewed the three Kendrick brothers—masterminds behind movies such as *Fireproof*, *Facing the Giants*, *War Room*, and, most recently, *Overcomer*. They have been *tearing it up* in their field, and yet years ago, before they got their start, the last thing they thought they'd be doing now was producing "Christian films." They wanted to be big Hollywood producers, but their mom, a faithful Christian, prayed them down a different path. During our interview, Alex Kendrick made a statement that sticks with me still. Referring to the day when he and his brothers decided to pursue filmmaking that honors Jesus, he said, "We vowed to chase the favor of God."[2]

Chase the favor of God.

For the Kendrick brothers, this hidden principle led to movies that would gross upward of $85 million each. Now I'm not saying that following God and his favor for you will lead to your getting rich. If you have traveled around the world, then you *know* it doesn't work like that. What I *am* saying is that as you are faithful to follow God's grace and favor, you will have all you *need* to accomplish his work. Yes, you may *need* millions of dollars to pull off a mission he has for you. Or what you *need* may look like this:

The motivation to start a new business or nonprofit.

The courage to adopt a child or mentor a teen.

The passion to help lift people from poverty who are struggling just like you did.

The encouragement to prevent someone from taking his or her life.

REFLECTION

I don't know where God's provision will lead you, but I am totally sure of this: *He will provide for you exactly what you need to act on what he has graced.* Your part is searching out, aligning your life with, and surrendering to what God has predestined for you to do. His job is everything else, my friend.

Everything, *everything* else.

10

DREAM KILLERS

Hold fast to dreams, for if dreams die
Life is a broken-winged bird that cannot fly.

LANGSTON HUGHES

Do you know what is the most common reason why people fail to fulfill their God-given purpose, besides not knowing how to discover it?

It's that they allow it to be taken away.

Even for the most accomplished men and women, the "God-sized dreams" spoken over them can fail to come to fruition because of thieves who steal those dreams. I call these thieves dream killers, and while some of those killers are obvious, some are obscured from view. Still, what we don't know can definitely hurt us. We'd be wise to keep careful watch.

If there is a more fitting demonstration of how to over-come the dream killers that threaten to take us down than the Old Testament story of Joseph the Dreamer, I don't know what it is. You probably remember Joseph, from his "tech-nicolor dreamcoat" fame. If I had to name one person who fought for God's purposes in his life despite a ridiculous on-slaught of injustices, setbacks, and fears, it would be Joseph, the favored son of Jacob, the boy of the troublesome dreams.

Fly through the last fourteen chapters of the book of Genesis and you'll surely be entertained. Joseph's life reads stranger than fiction, and yet this stuff *really did occur.*

"When Joseph was seventeen years old," the text tells us, "he often tended his father's flocks. He worked for his half brothers, the sons of his father's wives Bilhah and Zilpah. But Joseph reported to his father some of the bad things his brothers were doing" (Gen. 37:2).

So right off the bat: problem one. Joseph's brothers couldn't stand that he was more loyal to their father than them.

Problem two? The brothers' dad liked Joseph best.

"Jacob loved Joseph more than any of his other children because Joseph had been born to him in his old age. So one day Jacob had a special gift made for Joseph—a beautiful robe. But his brothers hated Joseph because their father loved him more than the rest of them. They couldn't say a kind word to him" (vv. 3–4).

Sibling rivalry runs *deep*, doesn't it? It certainly did for this bunch.

"One night," verse 5 says, "Joseph had a dream, and when he told his brothers about it, they hated him more than ever."

This dream was part one in a two-part vision involving Joseph seeing his family bow down to him someday. Joseph's eleven brothers especially had had it with what *they* would describe as his pompous attitude, his preferential status, and his dumb coat. "We know what we'll do!" they said to each other. "We'll kill him."

Thankfully, a cooler-headed brother in the group (somewhat) prevailed, and instead of murdering the youngest of their family, the brothers threw Joseph into a cistern, a deep well. Better plan. Not *great*, admittedly. But better.

Just as the brothers were wiping their hands of their brother, they noticed a caravan happening by, a group of traders with an abundance of goods.

They could use some goods, they thought. They knew just what to do. In exchange for some money, they sold their brother Joseph as a slave to the Midianite traders, who said they were headed to Egypt.

Upon reaching Egypt, Joseph was handed over to the captain of the guard of Pharaoh's palace—a man named Potiphar. And that was that. The brothers had gotten rid of the nuisance. Nobody had been killed. Joseph would be *fine*, they were sure. Excellent! On with life.

Dream Killer #1: Family

The first obstacle we face when trying to stay the course in pursuit of God's purpose for our lives is, in a word, *family*. Family! Can't live with 'em; can't get rid of 'em—am I right?

I'm just joking.

But Joseph's brothers weren't joking.

During my teen years, my mom and I began having a tough time. My childhood was *amazing*, but somewhere along those teen years, she and I clashed. I'm not sure if it was because we were similar in some ways, or because I was becoming more independent, or because I was just getting older. Whatever the reason, it was hard. She would have moments where she would black out and just start calling me names. "You're stupid. Why would you do that? What kind of smart boy thinks like that? Why do you think you could ever do that?"

In times of stress, she would say all these things and more.

One day she would be a strong advocate for my dreams and talents and ambitions, and another day, she would basically say, "You're nothing."

It was so unlike her that I'd always feel hurt and shocked. Once I was an adult, at the height of this madness, I sat Mom down and asked her why she chose to speak to me this way so often. She broke down crying. She apologized to me and said, "Because my mother did it to me."

How many of us are victims of someone in our family whose childhood wounds never got healed? I've talked with plenty of people who've had similar experiences. A dad said something when a boy was eight or ten years old, and that *one piece of negative input* held him captive for years and years. A mom held back affection from her daughter during the daughter's formative years, and that girl grew up to be a woman who could neither give nor receive true love. A little boy learns from the men in his family that he must be strong, unyielding, tough. That boy becomes a tyrant of a boss, a hard-hearted husband, and a distant friend. People have refused to start the business, take the promotion, protect the marriage, love their children well, accept people who are different from them, welcome new neighbors with open arms, practice patience when strangers are frustrating, or pursue a relationship with God—all because they were weighed down by past wounds embedded deep down within them. A piece of advice for these and thousands of others: *It's time to graduate from the wounds of your family.*

When have *you* felt stuck because of a family member's influence on you? When have you felt like your family was trying to kill off something that mattered to you, in the same way that Joseph's brothers worked to kill his freedom, his future, his hope?

I've come to think of the memories, habits, and dynamics that weren't exactly uplifting as volumes on a bookshelf. While I couldn't always control when they popped out, fell to the floor, and opened to an unfortunate chapter, I *could* control what happened next, which is that I'd pick them up and slide them back into their place on the shelf. I couldn't erase those parts of my past I didn't especially enjoy, but I certainly didn't have to dwell on them. I didn't have to sit and stare at them all night long, and the truth is, neither do you.

It has taken me years with God, pastors, mentors, and even counselors to get to the level of clarity I'm about to exhibit with you, but here goes: *If your family is holding you back from God's best, you must choose God over them.*

Every. Single. Time.

Dream Killer #2: Friends

The second obstacle we will always face when trying to stay the course in pursuit of God's purpose for our lives is, in a word, *friends*.

After Joseph was sold into slavery, he executed his duties so well that he found favor with Potiphar, the leader in charge. Through a series of events, Joseph found himself in yet another predicament, once again being punished by those who didn't like him. He was slandered and thrown into jail. But while he was in jail, he discovered he had a God-given gift. He could interpret dreams.

Soon, two members of the king's staff were thrown into jail with Joseph and became his friends. Those men began having dreams but weren't sure what those dreams meant—until they told Joseph about them and he interpreted their meanings. "Your dream is a prophecy," Joseph told one of them, a cupbearer, "a prophecy that you'll get out of jail soon."

The friend was elated. He made a deal with Joseph: when I get out of here, I'll get you out too. But he failed to keep that promise.

Genesis 40 says, "[Pharaoh] then restored the chief cupbearer to his former position, so he could again hand Pharaoh his cup. . . . Pharaoh's chief cup-bearer, however, forgot all about Joseph, never giving him another thought" (vv. 21, 23).

Forgotten—that's how Joseph felt. That's what Joseph *was*. The deal that had been made wasn't upheld, and Joseph continued to sit in jail.

The lesson? Friends don't always do what they're supposed to do. Friends don't always do what they *say* they will do.

Yes, they may show up on one day, but will they show up *every* day? There are friends who are ride-or-die, and there are friends who will just let you die.

We'd better be careful when choosing our friends.

A mentor of mine once said to me, "If you hang around successful people, you'll become successful by accident."

Did you catch that? It will happen *accidentally*. The reason? Proximity.

Let me show you how this works.

William Isaacs is the cofounder of the Organization Learning Center at MIT, and recently he conducted a study that bore out these results:

> Dialogue is a discipline of collective learning and inquiry. It can serve as a cornerstone for organizational learning by providing an environment in which people can reflect together and transform the ground out of which their thinking and acting emerges.
>
> Dialogue is not merely a strategy for helping people talk together. In fact, dialogue often leads to new levels of coordinated action without the artificial, often tedious process of creating action plans and using consensus-based decision-making. Dialogue does not require agreement; instead, it encourages people to participate in a pool of shared meaning, which leads to aligned action.[1]

Dialogue often leads to new levels of coordinated action. In other words, if you talk with someone long enough, you'll start to *move like them in the world*. It is woven into our biology to become who we hang out with most.

147

Think about it: You may have vowed never to become like your parents, and yet as an adult, you're just like them. You said you'd *never* act a certain way that your mom or your dad acted, but once you had kids of your own, you started doing those very same things. How does this happen? Proximity. When we have close proximity to someone, we engage in dialogue with them. When we have consistent dialogue with someone, we begin to think like that person thinks. When our thoughts align with another's thoughts, we begin to act the same way they act. Proximity leads to coordinated action every . . . single . . . time.

And this happens how? Yep, by accident. I ask you: Who are your friends? Who have you chosen to hang around most? Show me those people, and I'll show you who you'll become. Not on purpose, mind you. But by *accident*.

Dream Killer #3: Focus (or the Lack Thereof)

The third obstacle we will always face when trying to stay the course in pursuit of God's purpose for our lives is this: *focus*. Or, as Freddie Hendricks would say, the *lack* of focus.

Let's back up and look at how Joseph landed in jail to begin with.

When Joseph first arrived at Pharaoh's palace, he was made a servant. Even so, for a while, things were fine. Joseph had been graced by God to find favor with his master, and over time, Joseph climbed the ranks. But things took a turn for the worse when his master's wife approached Joseph one day. Her offer wasn't a subtle one: "Sleep with me, or else . . ."

148

Surely this pitiful slave would consent to the idea; what other plans could he possibly have? And yet the moment they were alone and she came on to him, she realized her plan had failed.

To make his escape, Joseph had to slide out of his coat and bolt, leaving Potiphar's wife standing there holding his garment. At that point the wayward woman must have thought, *Aha! A contingency plan.*

To get back at Joseph for rejecting her, the woman told her husband that it had been *Joseph* who made advances toward *her*, instead of the other way around. For his apparent wrongdoing, Joseph was thrown into prison by the same master who had once sung his praise.

Now it would be easy to skim past this part of the story, thinking, *Got it: crazy lady tries to wreck a man's life; man gets accused of something he didn't do; man does time for that thing . . . right.* But let's slow down for a second and think about how *you'd* feel. You were left for dead by your brothers, only to be pulled from the well they'd thrown you in and sold off in exchange for some silver coins. You made your way to Egypt and Pharaoh's palace, which isn't so bad, except that you're working there as a slave. You have no freedoms afforded you, except for the ones you eventually earn. And now you're tossed into prison for *doing the right thing*, and who knows how long you'll be there. I ask you, how would *you* feel?

Misunderstood? Forsaken? The victim of an unjust turn of events? Frustrated? Enraged?

Hopeless? As though life as you knew it was done? Joseph just took it in stride. God's purposes for him were bigger than this setback, and God would work it out in the end.

149

. . .

When Freddie Hendricks made me stare at that water bottle for twenty minutes, he understood something that I myself did not yet grasp. He understood the power of focus. "If you can learn how to focus," he told me again and again, "you can do anything in life."

Joseph was *so committed* to honoring God with his life, and also to honoring the leaders who he believed were placed in authority over him by God, that he was willing to give up everything to uphold that commitment. That is called *focus*.

To this issue of focus, a few questions, if I may:

Are you always jumping from idea to idea, or do you finish what you start?

Are you known for keeping your word?

How long can you read without stopping?

Do you ever *finish* a book?

Are you often late?

What about spiritual disciplines—how often do you pray?

When you sign up to serve at church, do you actually show up? On time?

Do you stay for the *entire time* you committed to serve?

Did you keep the last promise you made to God about putting the drugs down?

What about saving yourself for marriage?

Are you the type to get right up on the line and then stop?

What's the last sin you promised God you would stop doing? Did you stop? Are you still abstaining from that sin?

What's the last thing God instructed you to do? Did you do it? Are you still doing it today?

What do all these questions reveal? Our level of *focus*. Many people get to the finish line of fulfilling God's dream for them but never cross it due to a simple lack of focus. You were doing *so* well and then something shiny caught your eye. A year later, you're still stuck in the same place, wondering why you haven't made progress yet. Could it be that God has been waiting for you to follow through before he takes you to the next level? We complain about God not speaking to us, about God never showing us a vision of what he wants for our lives, but I have to wonder: Is the problem with God or with us?

Dream Killer #4: Fear

The fourth and potentially greatest obstacle we will always face, when trying to stay the course in pursuit of God's purpose for our lives, is *fear*.

Have you ever heard of the Random Fear Generator? If not, google it, and you'll find a pretty entertaining way to kill time while you're waiting for the gas pump to do its job. You couldn't or wouldn't *believe* the number of fears that exist, and the specificity of those fears. For instance, there is an actual name for the fear of being laughed at—*gelotophobia*. Yeah, that's what it's called. Or how about the fear of germs and dirt? *Mysophobia*. There's *nomophobia*, which is surely on the rise these days, since it's the fear of being out of mobile phone contact. And *osmophobia*, the fear of bad odors. I even saw something called *androphobia*, the fear of men, and wondered, can you have a particular fear if you, in fact, are the object of that fear?

Regardless of whether you have any of these fears, you most likely are afraid of something. The top two fears of the human experience are the fear of death and the fear of public speaking. And most of us don't stop there. Nearly every person I know has a few they could add to the list, which brings me to my question: What are *you* afraid of?

You may be afraid of heights. Or of flying. Or of the dark.

You may be afraid of failure. Or of being excluded by friends you love. Or of living life alone.

Our buddy Joseph probably understood fear. Though the text doesn't explicitly say it, didn't Joseph *have* to experience fear? Was he afraid of being killed? Of being ostracized from family and friends? Of a whole new environment—one in a totally different land? Was he afraid of what people thought of him after Potiphar's wife spread rumors and lies? Of being in prison? Or of God not rescuing him?

We don't have to stretch our imagination too far to envision a scene wherein Joseph's *fear* keeps him from pursuing God's purposes in his life. And yet, what a travesty that would have been . . . so much resolution the man would have missed.

It wouldn't surprise me to learn that Joseph at least feared Pharaoh. Pharaoh was known to be a savage executioner with a capricious style and a short fuse. This is why he was able to throw his most trusted servants into prison with barely a second thought. And yet God would use Joseph to penetrate Pharaoh's tough exterior during a time when Pharaoh needed help the most.

Back to the Genesis text.

Two full years had passed since Pharaoh released the cup-bearer from jail, and now Pharaoh was the one having odd dreams. In an attempt to get them interpreted, he "called for all the magicians and wise men of Egypt," but when he told those wise men his dreams, "not one of them could tell him what they meant" (Gen. 41:8). The story continues:

> Finally, the king's chief cup-bearer spoke up. "Today I have been reminded of my failure," he told Pharaoh. "Some time ago, you were angry with the chief baker and me, and you imprisoned us in the palace of the captain of the guard. One night the chief baker and I each had a dream, and each dream had its own meaning. There was a young Hebrew man with us in the prison who was a slave of the captain of the guard. We told him our dreams, and he told us what each of our dreams meant. And everything happened just as he had predicted. I was restored to my position as cup-bearer, and the chief baker was executed and impaled on a pole."
>
> Pharaoh sent for Joseph at once, and he was quickly brought from the prison. After he shaved and changed his clothes, he went in and stood before Pharaoh. Then Pharaoh said to Joseph, "I had a dream last night, and no one here

n tell me what it means. But I have heard that when you hear about a dream you can interpret it."

"It is beyond my power to do this," Joseph replied. "But God can tell you what it means and set you at ease." (Gen. 41:9–16)

Oh, how the tables had turned! And now Joseph had a decision to make. Would he stand and be confident in God, or would he cower and run in fear?

Joseph chose faith over fear. He stood tall in the face of the most fearsome leader in that region by leaning hard on the power of God.

• REFLECTION •

I ask you again: What are you afraid of?

Are you afraid of change? Maybe you know you need to improve, or grow, or allow transformation to have its way, and yet you're so at home in your circumstances, even if those circumstances are bad, that you are utterly terrified to move forward. You're stuck in the status quo. And so you self-medicate to avoid dealing with all that it will take to become the person you long to be.

Or maybe you're afraid of staying the same. What if you never get over this struggle? What if the relationship never heals? What if the dynamic never gets better? What if you can't find the courage to change? Maybe you're afraid of what others will think, afraid that in their estimation you just don't measure up.

No matter what your fear is, know this: if Joseph had crumbled under the weight of fear as most of Pharaoh's men did, he would not have been able to properly understand and fulfill the dream that God had designed to become his reality. For shortly after Joseph interpreted Pharaoh's dream correctly, Pharaoh put Joseph in charge of the entire land. Joseph's brothers would eventually need food during a famine and would have to ask Joseph for his help. They did end up bowing before Joseph, just as Joseph's original dream declared.

PART THREE

CHANGING THE WORLD FOR GOOD

11

A GREATER STORY

When your story connects to God's
story, it leads to a greater story.

JEFF HENDERSON

My friend who is an atheist and I got into an argument—a very hurtful argument. The kind of argument that makes you wonder if you should stay friends, despite five years of friendship logged. The inciting event was that my friend read something about Christians using religion to take advantage of the poor and decided that this awful claim was true of *all* Christians. "Christians are crazy," she said to me. "They're all manipulative."

Here's the statement that hurt the worst: "Sam, I thought you were smarter than to be part of a group like that."

I said something equally unkind to her, and then we disconnected the call. Without even saying goodbye.

At the center of our disagreement was this idea: "If God is so great, then why doesn't he solve all the problems that need to be solved now? Why do we have to wait until Jesus returns before things get better down here?"

Not long ago, during a trip to London, a group of pastors and I were able to spend time in the presence of one of the greatest living theologians of our time, N. T. Wright. During a Q&A session at the end of Wright's lecture, I stood and said, "It's an honor to be with you, sir. What you've done for the faith of my generation is truly astounding. One question: Why does God allow suffering instead of fixing everything now?"

I didn't record Mr. Wright's response verbatim, but I will tell you that his answer fell in line with the answers I've received over the years, as I've traveled the world asking the greatest minds in Christianity this same question on my show. Doctors, professors, speakers, influencers, you name it—I asked them all why God allows suffering, why God doesn't fix stuff that's broken, why God doesn't *intervene*. And the responses I've received fit into two main categories of thought. Let me give them to you here:

1. We just don't know—that's a very honest response, by the way—but we don't have to know why, to trust God. God is good, which means that everything he does or does not do reflects that goodness. Even what we deem to be bad, God is working for ultimate good. We don't have to understand God's

ways to believe that he exists and to trust that his ways are right. Trying to understand God's ways is like a toddler trying to understand every decision his or her parents make. There is much we simply can't understand.

2. God never promised us perfection in this temporal reality, but rather that he'd be with us in the imperfection and give us strength to make it through. Perfection is reserved for eternity with him, when every last tear will be wiped away. As we commune with the Holy Spirit, we will see glimpses of that redeemed reality here on earth, but that redemption will not unfold fully until the time of Jesus's return.

These conversations have led me to a core belief, which is that being a Christian who walks by faith requires becoming content with the unknown and trusting a good God you won't always understand.

This line of thinking wouldn't satisfy my atheist friend, but it definitely satisfies me. I wonder, is it enough to satisfy you? Think of it: It isn't *logical* to believe in a Savior who died for us on a cross, descended into hell for our sin, and rose again on the third day to rule and reign for all time. Such belief requires serious *faith*. You can't go headfirst into that line of thinking; you've got to go *spirit-first*.

Further, it isn't *logical* to love your enemies.

It isn't *logical* to give away your money.

It isn't *logical* to forgive those who hurt you.

It isn't *logical* to lay down your will and serve God.

We who walk with Jesus walk entirely by nothing but faith.

• • •

"Sam, we have to tell the Steve Harvey story on a Sunday here at Gwinnett Church—how Steve fibbed and didn't tell you he'd found your mother and then surprised you on national television by having her come out." It was my buddy Jeff Henderson talking, lead pastor of North Point's Gwinnett campus. Our church was in the middle of a series called "Cast Member," which positioned God's master plan for his followers as something of a movie and those followers as cast members filling the various roles. Jeff's point was that someday, after this world is redeemed, we'll all be able to look back on the scenes that confused us and see how they fit into the overall narrative arc. "God has a part for you to play!" Jeff told our congregation. "A part written *just for you* before the creation of the earth. The question that remains is, will you play it?"

Then he'd chant that line that has become my mantra: "I hope you will! Because when your story connects with God's story, it leads to a greater story."

"I'm in," I told Jeff that day he suggested I tell my story to our church. "Name the date, and I'm in." What I couldn't have anticipated was that in preparing for that preaching experience, I'd see my story in a whole new light.

My biological mother had three young children already when she found out she was pregnant with twins. She was extremely poor, and the father of those babies was long gone. What was she to do?

Her first instinct was to give us away, which I'm sure was a difficult conclusion to draw. But a twenty-one-year-old who is drowning in her circumstances will do anything to catch a break.

A man and his wife who had both been divorced, abused, broken, and lost discovered they couldn't have kids. She was forty years old; he was fifty-two. The solution? They would adopt.

The couple flew from DC to Georgia, where the lady who was running the adoption agency said, "You two just got married. You just became Christians. You're wanting a second chance at life. Do I have this right?"

The couple nodded their heads.

"Then you simply can't adopt those two babies. Given where they come from, they won't amount to much."

Cocaine. Addiction. Poverty. Welfare. Prostitution. Hopelessness. Pain. *You don't want those two babies. You'll be better off with someone else . . .*

My parents prayed. They talked. They prayed and talked some more. "No," they told the agency director, "there's something special about them. We pick those two babies. We want those two babies. We believe those two babies are ours."

Praise be to God.

Sara went on to get straight As from kindergarten through the twelfth grade. She won a dual scholarship to Spelman College and Georgia Tech and became an industrial engineer working for some of the largest multimillion-dollar consulting firms in the world.

Praise be to God.

By the tenth grade, I was playing six instruments—self-taught on all of them. I landed my first record deal at age sixteen. Alongside Freddie Hendricks, I started teaching on a collegiate level at age seventeen. By age twenty, I had written ten original musicals with Freddie Hendricks and had begun producing and recording songs for some of the biggest names in music, one of which hit the top twenty on Gospel Billboard. I started a nonprofit that reached more than one hundred thousand kids in a year. Went to ministry school to become a pastor. Spoke to half a million people on stages all across the globe. Launched a national TV and radio podcast interviewing the most influential voices in Christianity that is currently in one hundred million homes weekly. Wrote a book that was picked up by one of the largest Christian publishers in the world.

Praise be to God.

At age twenty-four, Sara agreed with our dad's decision that it was time we found our biological family. Dad always had *The Steve Harvey Show* on at the barbershop. "Steve Harvey could help us," he said. Sara wrote the letter that set the wheels in motion. Producer Dorothy started work at her new job and had more than one hundred story pitches thrown on her desk on day one. Our story happened to be on top. She called to see if we were interested. Sara said no . . . then recanted and said yes. The show hired a private detective to find our mother. They flew us to Chicago. They said, "Sorry, but no luck."

The show came back from a commercial break. Steve said, "Elinor, come on out." We met our mom on national television—after twenty-four years apart. Our siblings then were welcomed to the stage: Erica, Jarell, Lashawn.

We learned that when we were twelve months old, our mother tried to get us back. We'd already been adopted by then, but she *tried to get us back*. We'd never been abandoned, as we'd once believed. We'd been *wanted*, by two different moms.

I stewed for *weeks* over all that I'd missed with Elinor, and with Erica and Jarell and Lashawn. "Bro, you didn't miss a single thing," Jarell told me. "God *rescued* you from this life."

Jarell went on to tell me that throughout his entire childhood, Mom always had at least five grand worth of drugs on her person that she was dealing to afford food for her kids. "We would go days and days without eating," he told me. "It was hardly what you'd call a *life*."

He told me about our granddad, about the double life prison sentence, about dying in the hole. He told me about our uncles who were running from the law or dead. He told me about how hard things had been and about how I'd been blissfully spared.

Bro, you didn't miss a single thing. God rescued you from this life.

Praise be to God.

Praise be to God.

All praise be to the one, true God.

Before the creation of the earth, God wrote a part for you to play in the story of redemption he's telling day by day. The question that remains is, will you play it?

Will you play the part that's yours alone to play?

-------- • **REFLECTION** • --------

The greatest decision you could ever make in life is to become who you already are. The idea of control is so hard for us to let go. We want to be in charge of our fate. But ultimately, I believe we aren't in charge. With the idea of a creator being the author of a Greater Story involving us, predestined, pre-written and ordained, could you release your control to ultimately fall in place? You may say no. But think about this. Wouldn't life be easier? I mean, if everything was already done for us, wouldn't that mean that once we fall in place, everything else will? Maybe our lives truly do begin to click when we align with what's already been designed.

12

THE ART OF SACRIFICE

There is no decision that we can make that doesn't come with some sort of balance or sacrifice.

SIMON SINEK

I'm a huge fan of the Harry Potter series. J. K. Rowling's work is filled with nuggets such as the following one, which is spoken by the wise Dumbledore upon Harry's admission of almost being sorted into the Hogwarts House of Slytherin: "It is our choices, Harry, that show what we truly are, far more than our abilities."[1]

So much of life hinges on a single choice. And on the single choice after that.

Are there people who choose a destination other than what God has predestined for them? Absolutely. Are there ple in the grave with books they were supposed to write, people they were supposed to save, companies they were supposed to launch? Yes, yes, yes—without a shadow of a doubt. This is the power of choice. Now you may say, "How can a loving God let us choose less for ourselves?" And I would say, "How can he love you and *not* let you choose?"

This is the problem with us playing God: We simply do not have what it takes. We contradict ourselves. We act selfishly. We say we want freedom and independence, even as we long to be somewhat controlled. "God, let me choose you!" we cry out to our Father. "Don't make me go against my desires! I want to have sex because I feel like it. I want to do what makes me feel good!"

Moments later, we cry out, "God, won't you please keep me from harming myself? I can't take this pain anymore!"

May I state the obvious here? We simply can't have it both ways.

Before time began, God solved this dilemma by giving humankind free will. He wants to purify and redeem us, but he wants us to *choose* that noble course. I've heard it said that "Love is not love without choice. Once love is mandatory, it is no longer love. It is slavery, and God doesn't want slaves."

What does God want, according to John 15:15? What God wants is *friends*.

What this means for you and me both is this: The ball is always in our court. God gave *us* the power to give *him* the power over our lives. The choice is always ours.

• • •

I've noticed over the years that whenever I talk with people about pursuing God's greater story for their lives, they want that story while at the same time not wanting to do what it will take to get it. They want to choose it, but they don't want what comes with that choice. And yet, as we've just discovered, that story doesn't get told in or through our lives unless and until we choose it. It is a love story, written by God, and love is always a choice. But to choose God's love is to forsake all other loves; in other words, sacrifice is required. Most people want nothing to do with sacrifice, with the choice to willingly lay down our lives. Even so, the greatest stories are told on the *other side* of sacrificial living, on the other side of selfless regard.

Lecrae had to sacrifice familial love to embrace God's greater story for his life. Billy Graham had to sacrifice personal safety to embrace God's greater story in his life. Andy Stanley had to sacrifice relational harmony to embrace God's greater story in his life. For Bishop T. D. Jakes, it was a stable home life; for Tori Kelley, it was passion for life; for Oprah, it was fair treatment in her industry; for Natalie Grant, it was fertility. Martin Luther King Jr. was asked to make the ultimate sacrifice in giving up his very life for the cause, but just *look* at what God has done through that one man's life. A greater story, indeed.

Peace. Safety. Security. Joy.

What might you be asked to forsake for the purpose of playing the role God is asking *you* to play?

• • •

In my own life, I see that I am where I am only because others said yes to the question of whether they were willing to sacrifice on my behalf. Without their volitional selflessness, this greater story of God doesn't exist. There is no Steve Harvey. There is no reunion. There is no transformation that honors God. Sacrifice creates the context for the miraculous—I am living proof of that.

Elinor sacrificed her longing to raise her own babies to give us a future and a hope.

Belinda and Lamar sacrificed their assumptions about having a perfect family by choosing to adopt—and to adopt *us*.

Our extended family sacrificed exclusivity by embracing Sara and me as their own.

Mom sacrificed her corporate career to help Sara and me thrive at school.

Freddie Hendricks sacrificed his time and resources to shape a punk kid into a responsible man.

Bishop Long sacrificed his time and money to take a chance on a new believer and lay a spiritual foundation in that kid's heart.

A music executive, Cappriccieo Scates, sacrificed his time and resources to save a young artist from self-defeat.

Dr. Angela Watkins sacrificed privacy and her own reputation to bet on the potential of a relative unknown.

Dr. Bernice King and De'Leice Drane sacrificed time and resources to launch a young leader into prominence.

Chris Green sacrificed time and comfort to understand a culture that was not his own.

Andy Stanley sacrificed control to invite a young black man to take his stage.

Belinda and Lamar sacrificed self-protection to prompt their twins to find their bio-mom.

My sister Sara sacrificed personal comfort by agreeing to go on the show.

Steve Harvey sacrificed time and resources to chase down Elinor.

Elinor and my biological siblings sacrificed emotional predictability by agreeing to meet Sara and me.

Pastor Jeff Henderson sacrificed time and platform to help me birth *A Greater Story*.

On and on the list could go . . . so many sacrifices on my behalf. Selfless choice after selfless choice, each of these people made, to make me who I am. Living God's greater story always comes down to a choice. But if this choice is so life-changing, so worthwhile, so redemptive every time, why don't more of us make it? Why don't we opt for selfless sacrifice at every turn?

• • •

To understand the battle we must win, in order to choose selflessness and sacrifice, we must understand how our spiritual enemy works. You see, our enemy, the devil, loves to prompt us toward the wrong choice. "Stay alert!" 1 Peter 5:8 reminds us. "Watch out for your great enemy, the devil. He prowls around like a roaring lion, looking for someone to devour."

Instead of surrendering to God, the devil wants us to *take charge of our lives*. Why? Because he knows as well as we do that *you and I make horrible gods*. Humans who insist on sitting in God's seat drive themselves crazy because, while the human brain and physiology are truly miraculous things, there are limits to what they can do. We were never designed to *carry* glory; we were designed to *give* it. Attempting to do what was never ours to do is our quickest path to destruction. "You are holy," Psalm 22:3 says, "you who inhabit the praises of Israel" (WEB).

God is holy.

By extension, this means that we are only holy when we are found tucked away in him.

So Satan longs for us to assume the "God" role in our own lives because he knows that in that attempt, we will mightily fail. What's worse, in taking over the position that is God's alone, we cut off God's access to us. When we insist on going our own way, we by definition are living in sin. And because of God's perfect holiness, he cannot abide those in sin. If God can't abide us, then he can't come near to us, and when God is at a distance, his purposes for us are too.

In Isaiah 14:12–14 we see a snapshot of how Satan came to be: "How you are fallen from heaven, O shining star, son of the morning! You have been thrown down to the earth, you who destroyed the nations of the world. For you said to yourself, 'I will ascend to heaven and set my throne above God's stars. I will preside on the mountain of the gods far away in the north. I will climb to the highest heavens and be like the Most High.'"

Believe it or not, Satan started as a shiny, faithful angel who lived with and communed with God. But then he got filled up with himself, thinking he was all that and so much more: I will ascend to heaven! I will set my throne above God's stars. I will preside on the mountain! I will climb to the highest heavens! I will be like the Most High!

I, I, I, I, I.

From the beginning of his defiance, he set his purpose not at anything life-giving or excellent, but rather at "steal," and "kill," and "destroy" (John 10:10). He was fighting for his own glory, despite all glory belonging to God. "I will not give My glory to another," says Isaiah 48:11 (NKJV). God is God, and on the glory front, I'm telling you, he will not share. But some of us must learn the hard way, and man, was Satan's way hard.

He set himself in opposition to God and single-handedly ushered in the arrival of Jesus, who would conquer him once and for all. That third part of any good story—the resolution—would come when Jesus was raised from the dead. More from Isaiah 14:

> You [Satan] will be brought down to the place of the
>   dead,
>   down to its lowest depths.
> Everyone there will stare at you and ask,
>   "Can this be the one who shook the earth
>   and made the kingdoms of the world tremble?
> Is this the one who destroyed the world
>   and made it into a wasteland?
> Is this the king who demolished the world's greatest
>   cities
>   and had no mercy on his prisoners?" (vv. 15–17)

In the end, Satan will be the object of laughter and ridicule. Which begs the question, "Why continue to torment people today, when you are fighting a battle you cannot win?"

I don't pretend to speak for Satan, but let me say this: some players just can't help but talk trash, even when their opponent has already won.

Let me tell you why I'm so committed to working with people to find their purpose, to surrender to that thing they can do day in and day out that will bring the most glory to God. I do this work because I have seen what happens when we depart from that course, when we go our own way instead of God's.

Invariably, we start playing for the team of our sworn enemy. We start seeking praise for ourselves. Success for ourselves. Glory for ourselves! And in that, we self-destruct.

You and I stay the course in pursuit of God's purpose for our lives to remind ourselves and anyone watching that in this game called life, we've picked our side. We've chosen our team. We've put a stake in the ground, and we will not be moved. We've aligned ourselves not with the forces that are sure to lose, but with the One who has already won.

We will not hold back.

We will not shrink back.

We will not be wooed to the other side.

We've gone all in on gathering glory for God—and God alone—so that ultimately his story can be told throughout the entirety of the earth.

· · ·

Whenever I talk with someone who has turned this corner I'm talking about, someone who has decided—and resolutely so—to surrender his or her life to Christ, I'm reminded of that scene from John 6 where Jesus is talking with his disciples about the death he must endure in order to fulfill the will of God. "I tell you the truth," he said, "unless you eat the flesh of the Son of Man and drink his blood, you cannot have eternal life within you. But anyone who eats my flesh and drinks my blood has eternal life, and I will raise that person at the last day" (vv. 53–54).

The disciples did not like this plan. This was their teacher, their Master, their friend. They were supposed to eat and drink their friend? Uh, no.

"I am the true bread that came down from heaven," Jesus continued. "Anyone who eats this bread will not die as your ancestors did . . . but will live forever" (v. 58).

The disciples looked at each other and said, "What is he talking about?"

But Jesus wasn't about to relent. "I'm telling you the truth," he essentially said, "even though some of you just won't believe."

And now, the moment of truth: "At this point," the text says, "many of his disciples turned away and deserted him. Then Jesus turned to the Twelve and asked, 'Are you also going to leave?'" (vv. 66–67).

To which Simon Peter, brave soul that he could sometimes be, said, "Lord, to whom would we go? You have the words that give eternal life" (v. 68).

Jesus holds the answers to life. Where else would we go?

• • •

What those disciples would come to understand in due time is what you and I and every other lover of God around the globe understands today: that sacrifice of Jesus's body and blood is our only hope in this world. The rescue that Jesus secured for us is the only reason that we are alive.

Connecting ourselves to God's greater story means that we recognize that "when we were utterly helpless, Christ came at just the right time and died for us sinners" (Rom. 5:6). It means we see this great act of love as "a sacrifice for us, a pleasing aroma to God" (Eph. 5:2). It means we are putting our trust in God to provide, believing that "since he did not spare even his own Son but gave him up for us all, won't he also give us everything else?" (Rom. 8:32). It means that we have ditched the hang-onto-your-life plan and have gone God's way instead.

That last idea is taken from Luke 9:24, which promises that "if you try to hang on to your life, you will lose it. But if you give up your life for my sake, you will save it." It's a verse I thought about recently when I came across a news headline that said a well-known televangelist had "renounced the selling of God's blessings," a practice he had espoused since a decade before I was born. Doubters are infuriated, wondering if he means it this time, since he's made similar renouncements along the way. And while I don't agree with the prosperity gospel theology, haven't you and I both done the very same thing? At least once, haven't we misappropriated the Word of God to satisfy our own ambitions?

176

Every person alive is guilty of trying to control things that God says are outside of our control. We're guilty of plotting outcomes that God says we should not plot. We are guilty of claiming knowledge for things that God says cannot be known. We are guilty for holding on with a ridiculously tight grip to what we think we're entitled to.

There is a better way. "Give up your life for my sake," Jesus exhorts us. "That is how to save a life."

Now if Jesus wasn't about to put his money where his mouth was, we might blow past his "helpful advice." But that's not at all the case. Our Lord was about to carry his own cross to Skull Hill, where he would die the most brutal of deaths.

Matthew 26 is one of those chapters in the Bible that I can't read without cringing and squinting my eyes. In verse 36 we find Jesus and his disciples heading toward an olive grove, a garden called Gethsemane, where Jesus told them to sit down while he excused himself to go pray. The text says that he tapped Peter, James, and John, and with his inner circle, headed away from the group.

In the presence of his most trusted friends, he then "became anguished and distressed," saying to them, "My soul is crushed with grief to the point of death" (vv. 37–38).

He asked them to stay close, to keep watch, to stick with him, by his side. Going a little farther into the garden, Jesus, now alone, fell prostrate before God. "My Father!" he cried. "If it is possible, let this cup of suffering be taken away from me" (v. 39).

How desperately he wanted out of this deal, and who wouldn't? To die is one thing. To know you're about to die—and in the manner Jesus faced—is quite another. We'd be begging God too.

The account in the Gospel of Luke says that Jesus was so distressed that God sent an angel from heaven to strengthen his Son. Jesus then "prayed more fervently, and he was in such agony of spirit that his sweat fell to the ground like great drops of blood" (Luke 22:44).

Coming back to himself—to his purpose in this earthly ministry from the start—Jesus then said, "Yet I want your will to be done, not mine" (Matt. 26:39).

I'm telling you: faithful to the end.

After returning to his friends and rebuking them for having fallen asleep (insert blushing, wide-eyed emoticon here), Jesus pleaded with his Father a second time. "My Father!" he said. "If this cup cannot be taken away unless I drink it, your will be done" (v. 42).

A second time, he returned to his men. A second time, he found them asleep.

A third time, Jesus went before his Father. Three times, he begged for relief. Knowing it was a futile request—knowing that this course was set—he went to his disciples and said, "Go ahead and sleep. Have your rest. But look—the time has come" (v. 45).

His time at last had come. All those occasions when the disciples wanted Jesus to power up over people, over the religious elite, over the political establishment, Jesus would simply say, "My time has not yet come."

Well, that was all changing. His time was officially here.

But if this was "his time," then why was he sweating blood? And being arrested? And dragged off to die on a criminal's cross? Why was he being humiliated? And beaten? And spat upon? Why was he being killed?

Was this the radical revolutionary they'd hoped for? *This* was to be the Savior of the world?

In this moment we see Jesus modeling for us what he would eventually ask us all to do. *Sacrifice.* Sacrifice, so that this world can be a better place. Sacrifice, in order to find God's best. Sacrifice, so that God's grand, redemptive plan can be realized throughout the earth.

Which begs the question, how well are we following suit?

• • •

It's worth noting that the most successful people I know— and by the grace of God I've been able to sit with world leaders, key influencers, and billionaires along the way—all have the same thing to report. Without exception, what they tell me is this: "Sam, the fulfillment I've known from things I've acquired can't begin to compete with the fulfillment I've found by helping someone else."

That sentiment sounds familiar, doesn't it? In Acts 20:35, Luke quotes Jesus as saying, "It is more blessed to give than to receive."

A statement from John comes to mind: "For God so loved the world that he gave . . ."

And another one, from Andy Stanley: "Don't make the mistake of believing that every resource that comes to you is for your consumption, alone."[2]

Give! Give! Give!

Keep in mind at all times that what God has entrusted to you might be for someone else.

——• REFLECTION •——

What I've noticed, time and again, is that the people who have committed themselves to letting God write their story, to pursuing God's purpose for their lives, to modeling themselves after the great sacrifice that God prompted in his Son, are the same ones who are eager to sacrifice deeply.

Trust God in this: Follow his Son's example in laying *everything* on the line for him. You will be blessed when you give. You will glorify God when you give. You will save lives when you choose to give.

13

FAMILY REUNION

You don't choose your family. They are God's
gift to you, as you are to them.

DESMOND TUTU

"Elinor, come on out!" Those were the words that Steve Harvey spoke that made everything suddenly get real. Twenty-four years after her departure, in walked Sara's and my biological mom. I looked at Steve and then looked at Elinor and then looked at Sara seated at my side. For so long, it had been just her and me, the two of us doing our best to make it in this world. Some adopted kids act out, believing their identity was in their abandonment. For Sara and me, adoption had the opposite effect; adoption made us work hard. We *wanted* to succeed. We *wanted* to make our adoptive parents proud. We *wanted* to leverage the second chance we'd been given. We *wanted* to get life right.

Whenever I screwed up—and, as I've disclosed, those times were frequent—the thought that chased through my mind was, *Sam, don't let Dad down.* What that meant to me was this: "This man and his wife took you in when you had nowhere else to go. Show him a little respect, would you? Don't fumble the ball on the fourth down."

But now, Sara's and my bond would need to broaden. New family was headed our way.

• • •

People often ask me what it was like to be on national television the first time I met the woman who birthed me. My answer is always the same: "It was like being frozen in time."

If you watch the clip on YouTube, you'll see that Sara and I quite literally froze. We tried to move but couldn't. My head dropped, and there it stayed. Ten thousand emotions flooded my consciousness. I had no idea which ones to keep.

Should I be amazed?

Should I be happy?

Should I be humbled?

Should I be grateful?

Should I be mad at Steve Harvey for lying about not finding her and having her backstage the entire time?

As Elinor made her way to the couch where Sara and I sat, I sensed God giving me a message: "Son, snap out of it. You're on national TV. We'll deal with these emotions later on. Go hug your biological mom."

I stood up and reached for my mom.

No sooner had the weight of this moment sunk in than Steve Harvey dropped another bomb in my lap: "Oh, and your siblings are here too. Erica, Jarell, Lashawn, come on out!"

Lord, how much can we take?

In a flash, Sara and I went from being "all we got" to being the youngest of five kids, all from the same mom, the same dad. We both stood to embrace the three who then came onstage, all five of us looking *exactly* alike.

"We've been looking for you all these years," Elinor whispered. "I've been looking for you all these years."

• • •

My mom, my dad, Elinor, my siblings, Sara, and me—the group of us convened after the show to eat together, to catch up, to *hang*. I learned that my biological mother had gone to school for health-care administration and was studying to be a nurse. She wanted Sara and me to be proud of her accomplishments, and truly, both of us were.

At some point there in our hotel suite, someone made a joke, and all five siblings laughed. As soon as we heard each other cracking up, our laughter was arrested, replaced by shock. *We all had the very same laugh.*

My brother and I talked about having the same bald head— "When did *you* lose it?" "Twenty-three." "Yep. Twenty-three for me too." And Lashawn and Sara stared at each other like they were each looking into a mirror. Identical as the day is long.

"I started a nonprofit a few years ago," my brother was saying, "for at-risk youth in sports . . ."

"What's it called?" I interrupted him.

"No Limits," he said with a grin.

It was eerie, the number of similarities we found, and yet there were plenty of differences too.

Sara and I had grown up in a Christian home in the suburbs of Atlanta; my siblings had grown up fighting poverty in the hood. As stories came tumbling out that night, I realized how blessed I'd been.

When my dad first proposed the idea of Sara and me finding our biological family, his motivation was simply that we know our roots, and to feel resolution in how life had gone. As my mom and dad and Sara and I made our way back home to Atlanta the following day, I bear-hugged good ol' Lamar Collier and said, "Thanks for making that happen, Dad. One of the best ideas you've had."

• • •

Every other year, the Colliers from all four corners of this country descend on a hotel in Miami, Detroit, Atlanta, or Santa Monica, depending on the year, for the purpose of catching up, hanging out, looking ahead, and enjoying a vacation at the family reunion. The locations have been set since before I was born, chosen for their proximity to the largest number of Colliers and Willises (Dad's mother's family) and quickly cemented in stone. By the time Sara and I came along, we were just whisked up by that fast-moving river and incorporated into its flow.

I can still conjure memories in an instant of being twelve years old and piling into a fresh rental car—Dad behind the wheel, Mom in the passenger seat, Sara and me in the back—and heading from Georgia all the way to south Florida. Officially, I think the trip took eleven hours each way, but to me, it felt like a million. To coop up a family for such a long time? Agony. Just kidding, we loved it! Every moment. It was Dad's thing that he passed down to us. I can't wait to do it with my kids.

Once in the car, the party began. Sara and I ate entire boxes of Twinkies and Little Debbie Oatmeal Pies while rocking out to whatever each of us was listening to on our portable CD players. Even with the volume turned up well past what Mom had approved—"Turn that down! You'll burst your eardrums!"—I could hear Mom and Dad's music filling the car—Motown's Greatest Hits, Luther Vandross, the Temptations, Marvin Gaye. After the batteries in our CD players pooped out, the sing-along would commence. Same songs, same order, every single time: "Ain't Too Proud to Beg," "My Girl," "Back Stabbers," "I Wish It Would Rain," "What's Going On," "Ain't No Mountain High Enough."

When we finally pulled into the hotel parking lot in Miami, Sara and I scanned the parking lot for cousins and favorite aunties and uncles. (We liked the crazy ones best.) We piled out of the car, carried into the hotel lobby by that beloved mass of humanity, and as usual, Mom rushed off with the "girls," giddy to be back together again. Someone handed Dad a Coke or a beer, depending on the mood, and off he went, with his many brothers and sisters and an assortment of extended uncles, great-uncles, and cousins, to sit in the hospitality room for the usual game of spades. My cousins and Sara and I created our oasis wherever the grown-ups were not. We'd hit the streets, the pool, someone's room, or even the hotel lobby, enjoying our critical mass.

As was our custom, the following day my parents and aunts and uncles and cousins and I—more than two hundred of us in all—rested and prepared for the massive evening ahead. The Willis and Collier Banquet—oh, what a night.

Someone had always gone to the effort of putting together a program, and my name was always listed there. My whole family was behind my Christian Usher dream. "Get up there, Sam!" they'd cheer. "Give us some songs."

"Sing Saaaaam!" Sara would taunt me . . . how she loved egging me on.

That banquet would go on for hours, ending only because the food had run out, and with full bellies and full hearts, we eventually disbursed and went to bed. The old people stayed in their rooms, while we young guns would hit the town. Walmart, Sonic, the local grocery store—it didn't matter where we went, as much as that we went there together, as one.

Those trips—those are *life*, you know? Beautiful, powerful times.

. . .

Every other year, we have reunited this way—not just physically, but spiritually and emotionally as well. And every other year, I have shaken my head in disbelief that these people kept their promise to me.

"You are one of us now"—Mom and Dad tell me that's what these same aunts and uncles and older cousins said the moment my parents walked through the door, an infant in each pair of arms.

"You are one of us now!"

It was a promise made, that I'd found my place, my home, my people, my loved ones, my kin. And all these years later, those extended family members continue to welcome me in. They continue to embrace me with unwavering love. They continue to keep their promise, which in my view is unprecedented.

. . .

If I could offer you a final word of encouragement regarding surrendering your story to God's greater story, it's that the feeling you have when someone keeps a promise made to you is the feeling you will experience every day. When you abandon your self-spun plans for your life and gratefully accept the plans that God has for you instead, you activate the promises that God has made for those who earnestly seek his will. He has promised that you will share his divine nature and escape the world's corruption (2 Pet. 1:4). He has promised you a future and a hope (Jer. 29:11). He has promised you power and strength (Isa. 40:29–31). He has promised that your suffering will not be in vain . . . that it will produce in you endurance, and character, and hope (Rom. 5:3–5). He has promised to give rest to your weary soul (Matt. 11:28–29). He has promised you peace of mind and heart (John 14:27). He has promised to supply all your needs from his glorious riches in Christ Jesus (Phil. 4:19). He has promised "overwhelming victory . . . through Christ, who loved us" (Rom. 8:37).

He has promised that nothing can ever separate us from his love. "Neither death nor life, neither angels nor demons, neither our fears for today nor our worries about tomorrow—not even the powers of hell can separate us from God's love. No power in the sky above or in the earth below—indeed, nothing in all creation will ever be able to separate us from the love of God that is revealed in Christ Jesus our Lord" (Rom. 8:38–39).

And as we lean into God's presence and power . . . I mean, lean so hard that if he were to shift his weight, we'd topple to the ground . . . we put those promises to work in our lives.

(By the way, worry not. You're good. God never shifts his stance.)

The apostle Paul wrote in 2 Corinthians:

As surely as God is faithful, our word to you does not waver between "Yes" and "No." For Jesus Christ, the Son of God, does not waver between "Yes" and "No." He is the one whom Silas, Timothy, and I preached to you, and as God's ultimate "Yes," he always does what he says. For all of God's promises have been fulfilled in Christ with a resounding "Yes!" And through Christ, our "Amen" (which means "Yes") ascends to God for his glory.

It is God who enables us, along with you, to stand firm for Christ. He has commissioned us, and he has identified us as his own by placing the Holy Spirit in our hearts as the first installment that guarantees everything he has promised us. (1:18–22)

God's promises for us are yes.

God's promises for us are *amen*, which means "let it be so!"

Funny story: I was interviewing Lysa TerKeurst for my podcast recently, and in response to one of my questions, she got so revved up that we had church right there on the show. I let her roll as long as she wanted to roll, and when she came up for air, I was hollering and amen-ing her left and right. This is a black church tradition, giving you an "Amen!" when you bring it strong. Why? Because we're wanting that thing you're preaching to be so, to be so, to be so!

What the Bible is saying is that when God makes a promise to us, he can't not keep it. His promises will be so,

> will be so,
> will be so.
> His promises are yes . . . and amen.

• • •

For three years, I've been using my TV and radio podcast to interview musicians, actors, celebrities, corporate leaders, pastors, speakers, and other influencers, and for three years, I've been blown away by the stories these people have told. I always kick off the episode by playing my guest's current favorite worship song . . . or, as was the case when I asked Andy Stanley for the title of his "current favorite worship song," he said, "Summer of '69." As in, Bryan Adams, circa 1988—the year I was born.

I cut to the song, and when those opening lines kicked in—"Bought my first real six-string. Bought it at the five-and-dime"—I thought Andy might never come back from his state of sentimental euphoria. The dude loves him some eighties soft rock.

Anyway, after the song I always, always do the very same thing. In nearly one hundred episodes, I don't believe I've deviated from this pattern even once. Here it is: I remind my guest of the accomplishments he or she has racked up in life—all the high points, all the victories, all the wins. And then I say, "But we know it didn't start there. Take us back to where it did begin, to the 'little' version of you, to you as a child, to you before all the growth and success. How did you get from there to where you are now? Give us the story of you."

And oh, the things I hear in response to that question.

"I grew up in a predominately Latino neighborhood . . ." the story begins.

Or, "I grew up in what you'd call a 'good home.'"

Or, "I grew up in Decatur, Georgia—Decatur, where it's greater!"

Or, "I grew up in the church. My dad was a pastor, so I guess you could say I was a typical PK."

Or, "I grew up in Bristol, Oklahoma, and was the kid who led outright revolts in elementary school over things like our needing chocolate shakes added to our school menu . . ."

From there, the drama builds as my guests explain the defining moments of their childhood and how their ability to cope with the challenges we inevitably stumble upon in life was influenced by that initial setting—the where and who and when of their earliest days. The challenges I've heard about have run the gamut: Poverty. Bullying. A parent's divorce. A learning disability. Fear.

Onto those first layers of personhood, life continued to build. Did they graduate from high school? Did they have interests outside of school? Did they have a circle of close friends, or were they loners? Were those enjoyable days for them?

What about college? If they did go, then where? Who paid for it? What were they hoping to gain from the experience? What did they gain as a result?

And looking back, what do they make of those first jobs they held? Did they love working or abhor it? Did they work for people of integrity or not? How did it feel to take home a paycheck? What did they spend their money on?

So many defining moments are attached to our relationships, and this certainly has been true for my guests. One guest chased his high school girlfriend (who had just broken up with him and was now chasing another guy) to Oklahoma for college, where he lives and ministers still today, three decades later. He and that girlfriend just celebrated thirty years of marriage and are as happy as can be. That one decision— chasing someone who said she wanted nothing to do with him to a school two states from home—changed everything for him.

One decision! And one that seemed like foolishness at the time.

Others speak of a distant or abusive father, a mother who taught them to love well, siblings who were ridiculously competitive, a doting teacher, a renaissance-man uncle, a coach who wouldn't let them quit. "That relationship changed the entire trajectory of my life," they tell me. "I'm who I am because of them."

Sometimes they mean this as a compliment to that key person; sometimes they don't. The point is, the relationship marked them. It confirmed something in their spirit—for good or else for ill.

The setting.

The initial character rundown.

And then those stories go here next: "You know, Sam, I always thought I was gonna . . ." They complete that sentence with every imaginable endeavor.

"I always thought I was gonna be a teacher . . ."

"I always thought I was gonna go into business . . ."

"I always thought I was gonna get married . . ."

"I always thought I was gonna move to the west coast . . ."

"I always thought I was gonna keep playing music . . ."

But then God. That's what they say next. "I always thought I was gonna . . . but then God . . ."

"I always thought I was gonna go into business, but then God met with me at a youth camp and called me into ministry."

"I always thought I was gonna be a teacher, but then God landed me a marketing job."

"I always thought I was gonna keep playing music, but then God stuck me in the role of a youth choir director!"

Here, by the way, is where I always lean in, to listen closely to what they say next. Because what happens next is the fork in the road, the point in the journey where they had to decide whether to follow where God was leading or to buck his way and do their own thing.

The funny thing about this particular fork? If they chose poorly at that first one, another one will show up. It's as if rebuffing God only makes God say, "Ah, got it. All right. I'll catch you a little farther up the road."

He is not willing that any would perish.

He is not desirous of any of us abandoning his will and ways.

He loves when his children pursue right living, which always involves his paths, his plans. But he will not force his way into our lives. He waits to be invited in. Remember?

And so, the forks: Will we go God's way this time? Or this time? Or this time? Some of my guests had racked up a dozen self-focused forks before they finally got a clue. And yet there God was, waiting patiently: "You in this time? Okay, good." From there, the story is a broken record. A deliriously delightful broken record. God did this . . .

And then God did that . . .

And then God opened this door for me . . .

And then God showed me that . . .

Tears spring to my eyes every time we get to this part. You are a good, good Father, God. Though I usually stay quiet as my guest recounts God's faithfulness in his or her life, inside I'm begging to know, "What happened next? And then? And then after that?" My appetite is insatiable for hearing what it's like to be living inside God's greater story. More precisely, my appetite is insatiable for living inside God's greater story. His goodness, his faithfulness, his kindness, his commitment to me. I can't believe the fulfillment I've known by going God's way instead of my own. Which makes me wonder, is this your testimony too? Is this the story your life will tell?

● ● ●

One time I asked my good friend Jeff Henderson to be on the show. Although Jeff is a lead pastor with North Point today, he comes from the corporate world and, as a former marketing exec for both Chick-fil-A and the Atlanta Braves, is incredibly respected there. Before I let him go, I asked if he would share one or two tips for people who are trying to get traction with a new business idea, a new product, a new side hustle, a new something that they hoped would gain liftoff in their life. Not surprisingly, Jeff was ready with suggestions galore, and one of the things he mentioned stuck with me for days and days after our chat.

He said, "If you can't tell the story of your idea or product in a short elevator ride, and tell it compellingly, then you've still got work to do."

Granted, Jeff was referring to the worlds of entrepreneurship and product development, but for me, the application that resonated most was that of us . . . our very lives.

What were your beginnings like? What is your original where, when, and who? What were you just sure you were going to do in life?

What was your but-then-God turn of events? What happened when you came to that first fork in the road? Did you surrender or go your own way?

Was there a second fork? A third fork? A fourth or fifth or sixth? What do you attribute your hard-heartedness to? What did it take for you to finally give way? For you to finally sacrifice?

And, finally, what has the journey been like for you since? What have you learned? What's been overcome?

If you're still staring down that first fork, wondering how on earth you got to this place, let me drape a loving arm around you and tell you that your life is about to get good.

If you will choose surrender, then God will thrust you into opportunities for transformation you never dreamed you'd have the privilege to know. He will give you the power to do what you can't do in your own strength. He will reveal the next steps as you go. He will carve out capacity for greater courage in you so that surrender will come naturally for you.

———• REFLECTION •———

Do you see your good, good Father, standing there, waiting patiently, arms lovingly outstretched toward you? He's rooting for you to set foot not on your path, but on his. Do so, and you're in for adventure. You're in for impact. You're in for peace.

Do so, and hear your heavenly Father whisper, "Ah, yes. Now we've got ourselves a story!"

• • •

I'd love to hear how this book may have impacted you. Overall I'd love to journey with you as you discover your greater story in God! Send me a message at stories@agreaterstory .org.

ACKNOWLEDGMENTS

I want to personally thank Ashley Wiersma, Susan "Sojourna" Collier, Alexander Field, and everyone in Baker Publishing Group's marketing and editorial teams for the blood, sweat, and tears they poured into the making of this book. You guys are truly game changers and ambassadors for the kingdom!

NOTES

Chapter 1 Family Matters

1. "Alicia Keys Says Her Pregnancy Is 'the Most Brilliant Gift,'" Music -News.com, July 21, 2010, https://www.music-news.com/news/UK/35 449/Read.

2. Diane Ackerman, *A Natural History of the Senses*, rev. ed. (New York: Vintage Books, 1995), 7.

3. Lucy Phelps Hamilton, "'If De Babies Cried': Slave Motherhood in Antebellum Missouri" (master's thesis, Pittsburg State University, Pittsburg, Kansas, 2015), https://digitalcommons.pittstate.edu/cgi/viewcon tent.cgi?article=1046&context=etd.

Chapter 2 Church Clothes

1. Tracy Jan, "White Families Have Nearly 10 Times the Net Worth of Black Families. And the Gap Is Growing," *Washington Post*, September 28, 2017, https://www.washingtonpost.com/news/wonk/wp/2017/09/28 /black-and-hispanic-families-are-making-more-money-but-they-still-lag -far-behind-whites/.

2. William Raspberry as quoted in "Turning the Corner on Father Absence in Black America," Morehouse Research Institute and the Institute for American Values, 1999, http://americanvalues.org/catalog /pdfs/turningthecorner.pdf.

3. "Turning the Corner on Father Absence."

4. "Turning the Corner on Father Absence."

5. "Father Absence + Involvement," National Fatherhood Initiative, accessed February 10, 2020, https://www.fatherhood.org/fatherhood -data-statistics.

6. Ana Swanson, "144 Years of Marriage and Divorce in the United States in One Chart," *Washington Post*, July 23, 2015, https://www.wash ingtonpost.com/news/wonk/wp/2015/06/23/144-years-of-marriage-and -divorce-in-the-united-states-in-one-chart/?noredirect=on.

Chapter 3 The Day My Life Became My Own

1. Associated Press, "Jordan Tries to Recapture Magic as Wizard," ESPN, October 1, 2001, http://assets.espn.go.com/nba/news/2001/0925/1255032 .html.

2. Sam Collier, "Brad Lomenick: Celebrating CATALYST, Determination, New Initiatives and His New Book," April 20, 2018, in *A Greater Story*, podcast, https://podcasts.apple.com/us/podcast/40-brad-lome nick-celebrating-catalyst-determination/id1183571837?i=100040935 2281\.

Chapter 4 The Road to Restoration

1. Marissa Evans, "Sharpeville Massacre," Blackpast, February 22, 2009, https://www.blackpast.org/global-african-history/sharpeville-massacre/.

2. I read about this study in Nir Eyal's great new book, *Indistractable: How to Control Your Attention and Choose Your Life* (Dallas: BenBella Books, 2019), 28–29.

Chapter 5 When Faith Is Tested

1. For more information about the "rhema word," visit https://www .gotquestions.org/rhema-word.html.

Chapter 9 A God Dream

1. I heard this quote from Bishop Jakes at the FOCUS 2010 Conference at New Birth Missionary Baptist Church on April 20, 2010.

2. Sam Collier, "The Kendrick Brothers: OVERCOMER the Movie, the Purpose of Christian Films, the Kendrick Journey," April 20, 2019, in *A Greater Story*, podcast, https://podcasts.apple.com/us/podcast/71 -kendrick-brothers-overcomer-movie-purpose-christian/id1183571837 ?i=1000447598700.

Chapter 10 Dream Killers

1. William N. Isaacs, "Dialogue: The Power of Collective Thinking," Systems Thinker, 2018, https://thesystemsthinker.com/dialogue-the-power -of-collective-thinking.

Chapter 12 The Art of Sacrifice

1. J. K. Rowling, *Harry Potter and the Chamber of Secrets* (London: Bloomsbury, 1998), 333.

2. "If Money Talked, Part 1: The Consumption Assumption // Andy Stanley," YouTube video, posted by Andy Stanley, January 30, 2020, https://www.youtube.com/watch?v=C43AvQ7gqLA.

Sam Collier is a pastor, speaker, writer, and host of the *A Greater Story with Sam Collier* TV show and radio podcast. He is a speaker and host at North Point Ministries, founded by Andy Stanley, and he also communicates nationally and internationally as a speaker and contributor to the ReThink Group, Orange Network, Orange Tour, Alpha International Leadership Conference, Willow Creek Global Leadership Summit, Culture Conference, and more. He has also been interviewed on numerous TV shows, podcasts, and radio programs. Collier lives with his wife, Toni, and their children in Atlanta, Georgia.

CONNECT WITH SAM

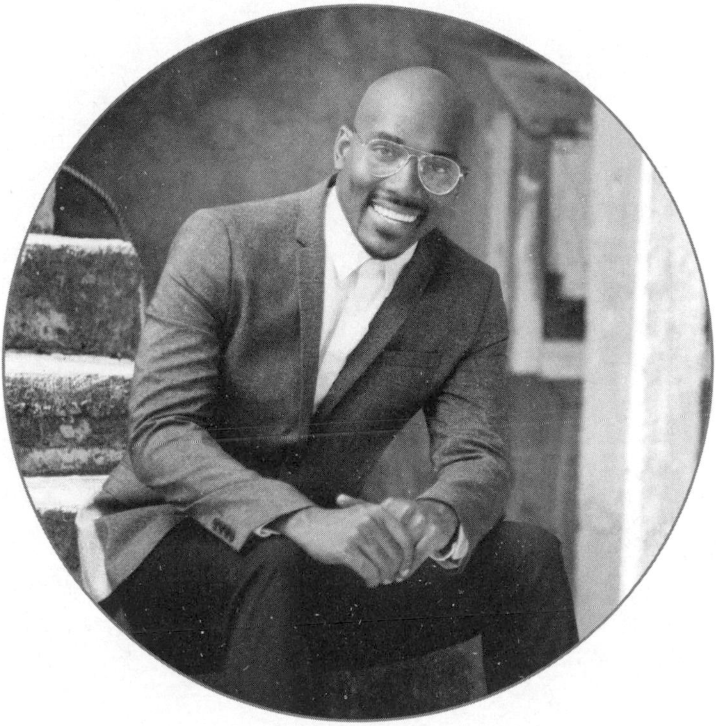

AGREATERSTORY.ORG

@SamCollier

TUNE IN TO
A GREATER STORY
PODCAST

Sam Collier sits down with top Christian influencers and celebrities to unpack their incredible purpose-filled stories and discuss current events, hot topics, and success tips through the lens of faith.

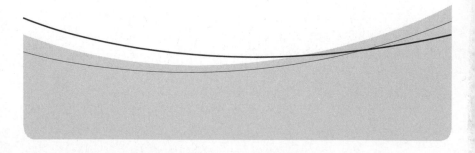